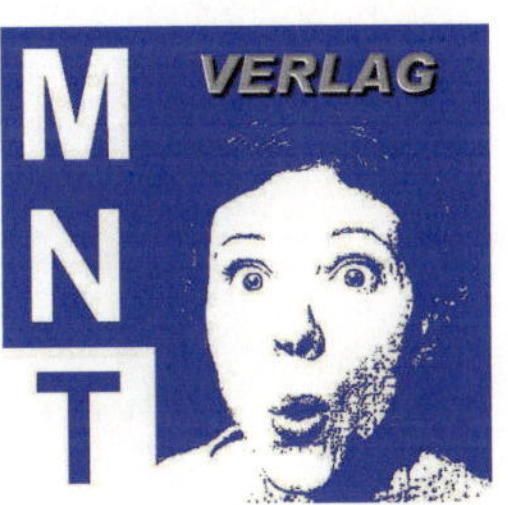

Roger Duhamel

CANADIAN ESKIMO ART

Development of Eskimo Carving

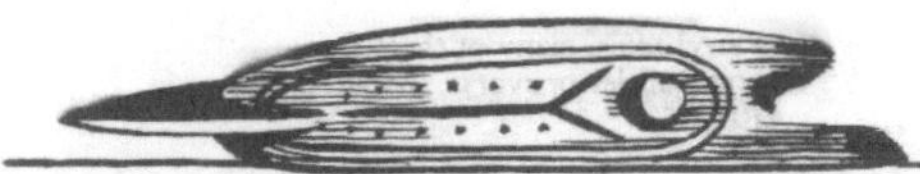

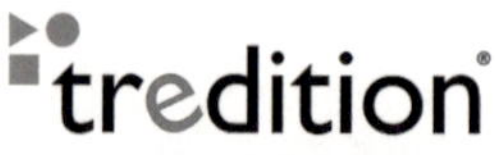
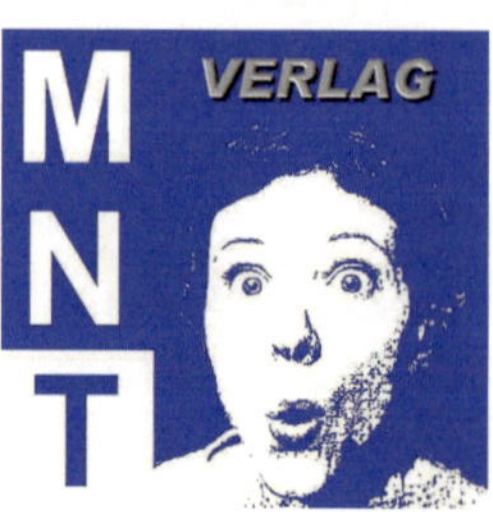

© 2010 MENSCH NATUR TECHNIK Verlag /: tredition GmbH
Printed in Germany
ISBN 978-3-86850-715-7

Bibliografische Information der Deutschen Nationalbibliothek
Die Deutsche Nationalbibliothek verzeichnet diese Publikation in der Deutschen Nationalbibliografie; detaillierte bibliografische Daten sind im Internet über http://dnb.d-nb.de abrufbar.

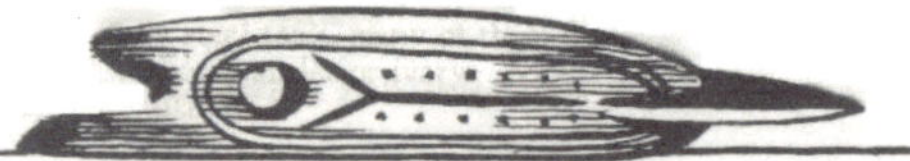

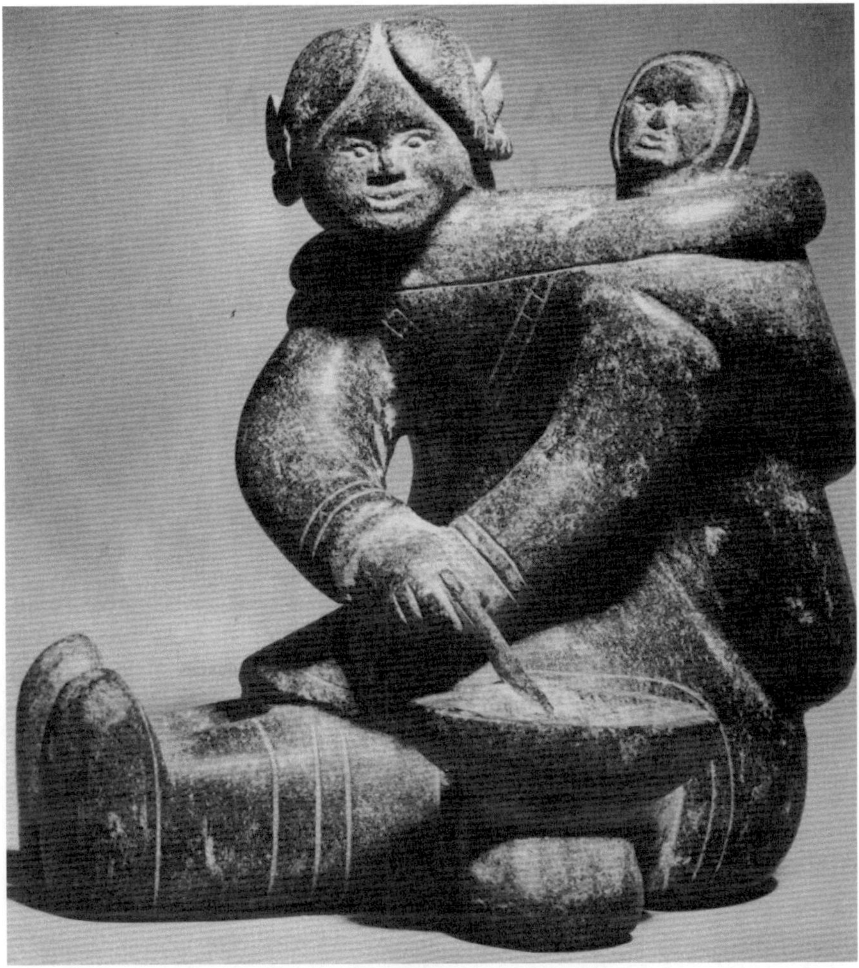

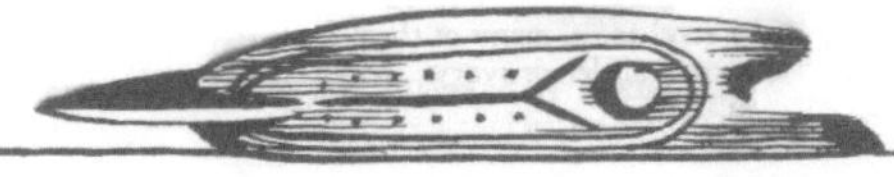

MOTHER AND CHILD KUNAMEE
CAPE DORSET, BAFFIN ISLAND

ARTISTIC EXPRESSION IN CANADA has taken many and varied forms because of the diverse elements from which our nation has been fashioned. The early French settlers, the British who followed them and more recent Canadians who have come from many parts of Europe and the world have all made their essential contribution to the cultural life of Canada. Few forms of artistic endeavour, however, have attracted wider public interest and enthusiasm, both here and abroad, than work of our Indian and Eskimo peoples. This booklet deals exclusively carvings of the Eskimos, a small but important group in the Canadian population.

Carving has always been an essential part of hunting culture of the Canadian Eskimos. With only natural resources such as stone, occasional pieces of driftwood and ivory and bone with which to make efficient hunting tools, Eskimos, of necessity, became accomplished carvers.

We may be grateful that this skill was not restricted to the manufacture of tools. Since early times, other objects have been carved. Perhaps for magical reasons, for success in hunting, for toys, for amusement, small figures of men and animals were carved in the round. Hunting and domestic scenes were also engraved on stone, bone and ivory.

This booklet outlines the development of Eskimo carving and shows the variations in form and subject of carving and other Eskimo crafts. Like the figures of animals, men and birds, all Eskimo handicrafts are characterised by simplicity and strength. Although all the work produced cannot be classed as art or sculpture, it never fails to provide a fascinating reflection of Eskimo life.

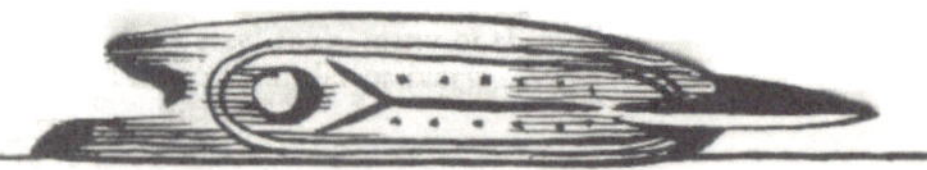

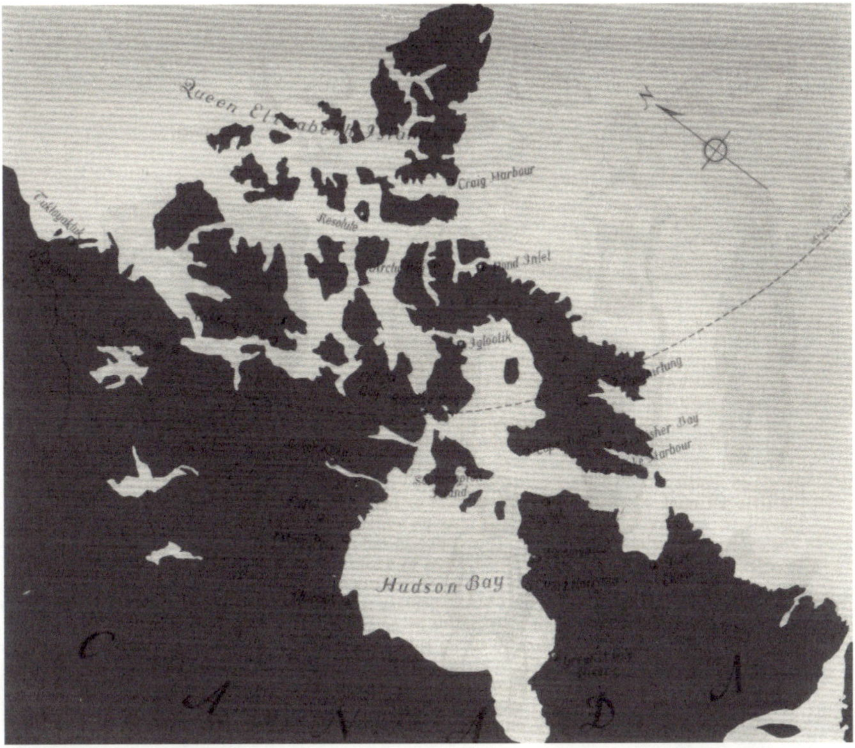

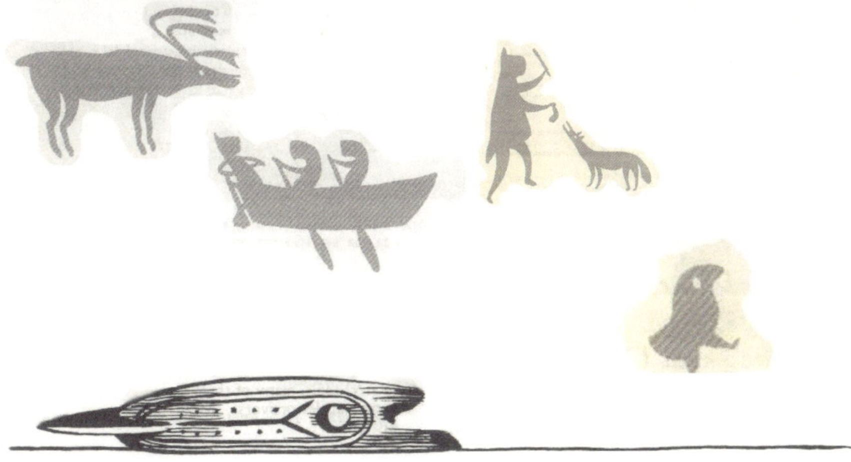

Queen Elizabeth Islands
Craig Harbour
Resolute
Pond Inlet
Tuktoyaktuk
Igloolik
Pangnirtung
Frobisher Bay
Harbour
Hudson Bay
C A N A D A

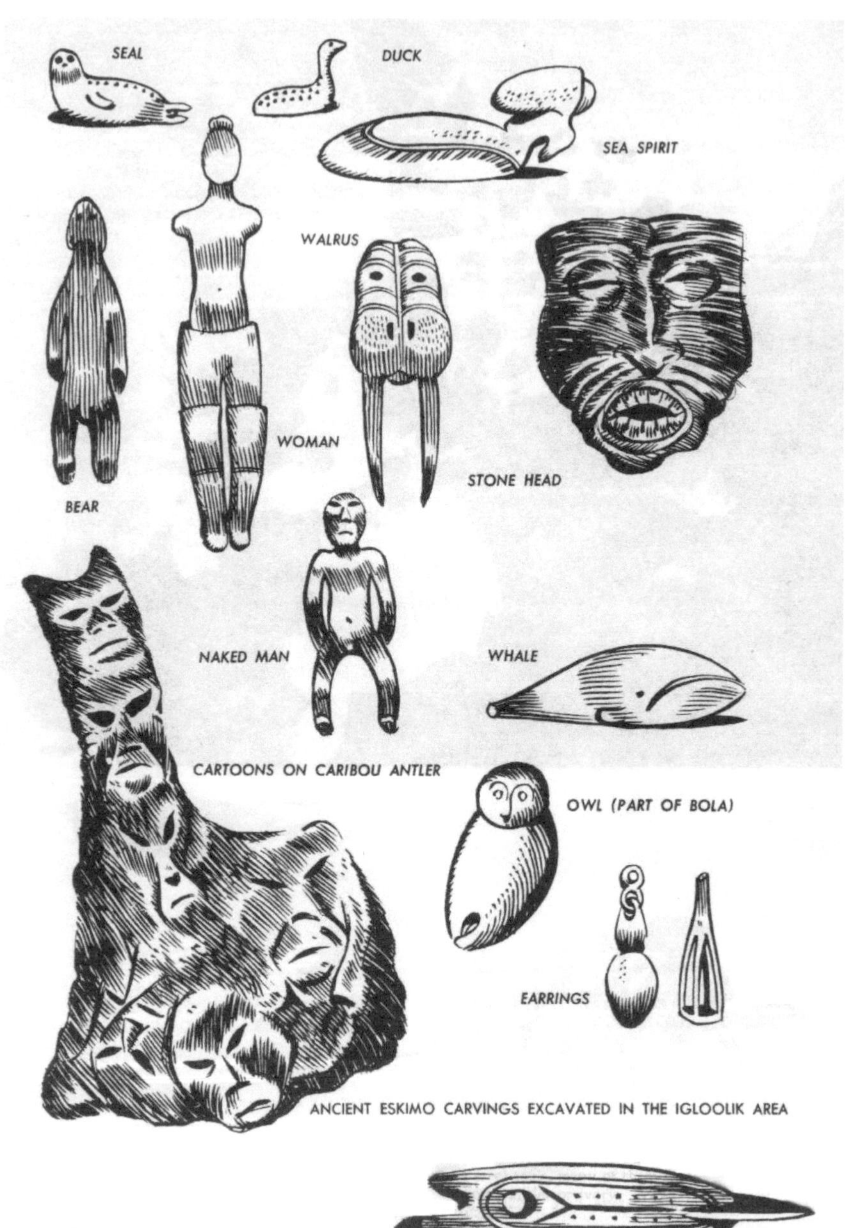

SEAL
DUCK
SEA SPIRIT
WALRUS
WOMAN
STONE HEAD
BEAR
NAKED MAN
WHALE
CARTOONS ON CARIBOU ANTLER
OWL (PART OF BOLA)
EARRINGS
ANCIENT ESKIMO CARVINGS EXCAVATED IN THE IGLOOLIK AREA

THE ESKIMO PEOPLE OF CANADA, cheerfully living a difficult existence in a hash climate, have developed over the centuries a unique art form, which today has won for them praise and acclaim wherever their work has been shown.

In an unceasing struggle for food and shelter, which has been their lot, with no wood but driftwood, with not textiles and no vegetable dyes, the Eskimos had few materials with which to create works of art. In consequence, they turned to the stones of their land, from which they were compelled to fashion their tools, as a medium for artistic expression. Out of the lifeless rocks they wrested imaginative and lively forms, depicting not only human beings and animals but also imagined creatures seen only in their dreams. Even today, after more than a century of exposure to European culture, this primitive art persists, original, creative and virile.

By force of circumstances these carvings have always been small. People, who are constantly on the move, pursuing game on which they must depend for the necessities of life, cannot burden themselves with large pieces of sculpture.

In the Igloolik collection of ancient carvings at Churchill, Manitoba, the figures are confined to such objects as human beings, animals or birds. Some of the animals are imaginary creatures, and sometimes human beings are portrayed in caricature. Similarly some of the utilitarian objects are decorated, but no decoration is allowed to interfere with the efficiency of the article itself. At Churchill, also, there is to be seen a caribou antler carved with cartoons of human faces. Antlers have been in this way by Eskimos in every part of the Arctic.

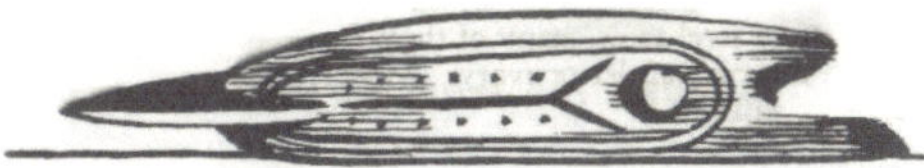

In decorative handicrafts the art forms employed as a rule are highly stylised and sometimes abstract. At the top of this page is an example of abstract design used in decorating clothing, or personal articles. At the bottom is a decorated harpoon head.

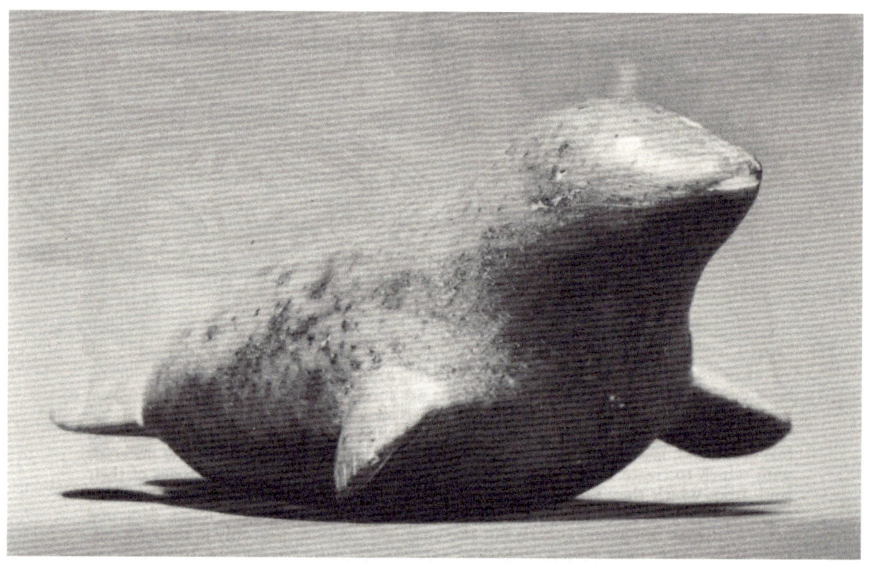

SEAL ON THE ICE BY KUDLALAK,
CAPE DORSET, BAFFIN ISLAND (SERPENTINE)

A MODERN SCULPTOR, asked to produce a work of art with nothing but the tools used by the Eskimos, might well be baffled. These people know nothing of mallet and chisel, they have no callipers or dividers. The Eskimo artist must make do with the tools used in daily life, for building his kayak, or for making his harpoons and stone vessels.

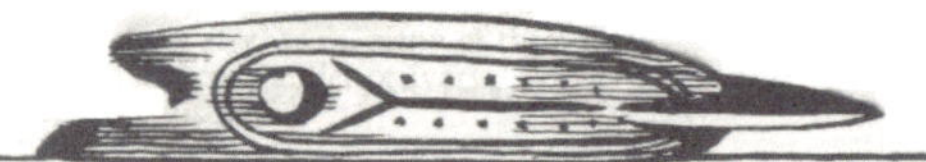

In the older cultures, the Eskimos shaped their tools by chipping them from fine-grained, flint-like stones which readily took a sharp edge. In later cultures, tools were also made from slate which was ground and polished to the form desired. Common to the both techniques, whether chipped or ground, were certain basic tools-adzes, hand drills, reamers and crude saws produced by chipping notches in the edge of a stone blade. Today most of these have been replaced by steel tools, many of them from scrap metal ground to shape and fitted in a handle of bone, antler or ivory. Modern tools, such as saws and files, are used when they are available.

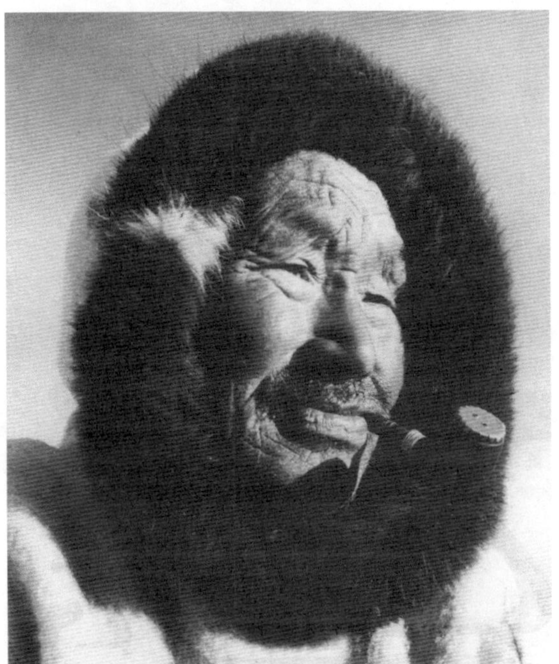

KUDLALAK, HUNTER AND CARVER
CAPE DORSET, BAFFIN ISLAND

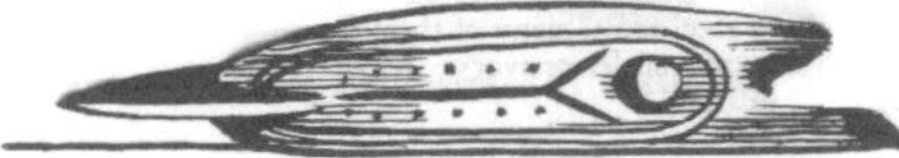

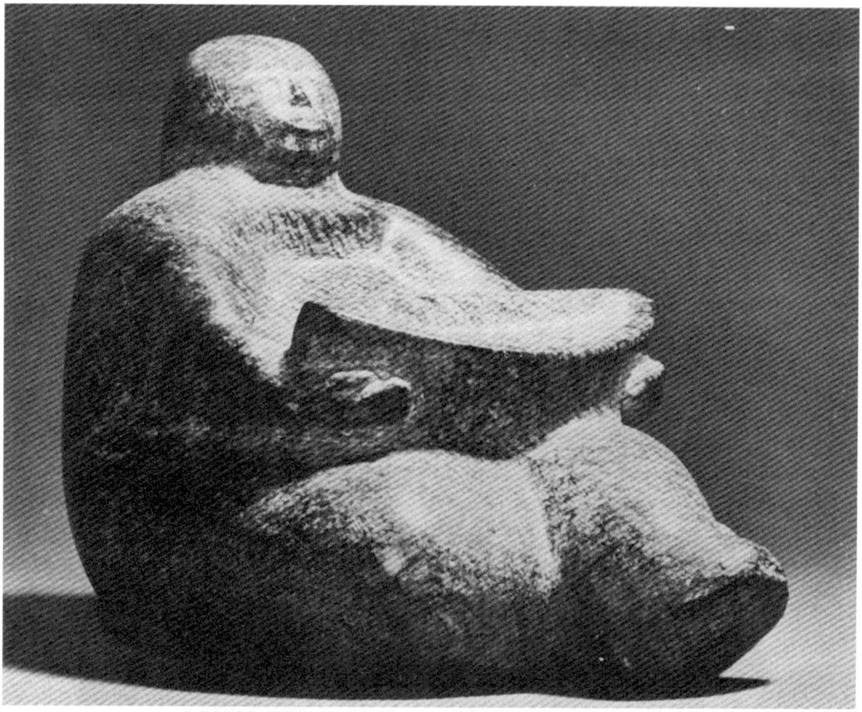

MAN WITH STONE LAMP BY SHOOVAGAR
CAPE DORSET, BAFFIN ISLAND

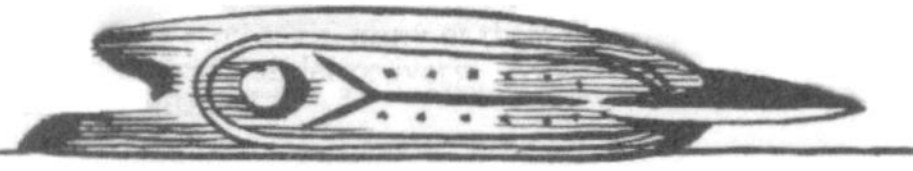

MANY ESKIMO PIECES tell a story of animal life: the owl guarding its nest, the bear followed by its cub, the struggling bird in the hands of a boy. The concept is always simple, the statement direct and vivid. The Eskimo carver has advantage of complete familiarity with the seals, the caribou, the walrus, the birds which he depicts. They are part of his life. There is seldom a day when he does not see one or more of these animals dead or alive, still or moving. The experiences of the hunt are a large part of his conversation, and his descriptions of them to his friend are illustrated with pantomime and mimicry for the diversion and information of his audience. His concept of the universe causes him to ascribe to things, whether living or dead, the emotions and even the speech of humans. It is not difficult for the primitive Eskimo to believe that the animals talk to his occasion, and when the narrative of the hunt is told and retold their conversations are as real to him as the rage of the harpooned walrus.

The human being, though, is at the centre of Eskimo's art. It offers the most in subject matter, for the lives of people are infinitely fuller and more varied than the lives of animals. The hunter stalking the polar bear, the mother holding the child, the boy solemnly dancing on his knees – these are the subjects which have appealed to native artists.

In his art, the Eskimo is expressing himself through the stones and ivory, the skins, the grasses which are the setting of sparse and barren tundra where he makes his home. Where nature permits, there art flourishes; but where the materials are lacking the Eskimo expresses himself in forms more transitory than the carvings which can be shown to the outer world.

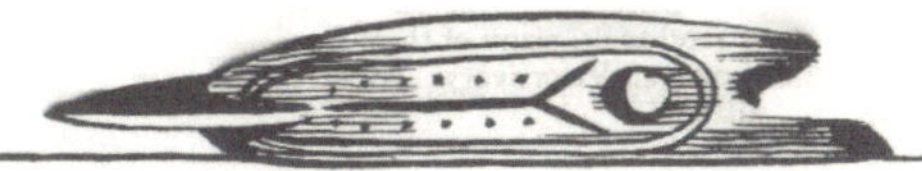

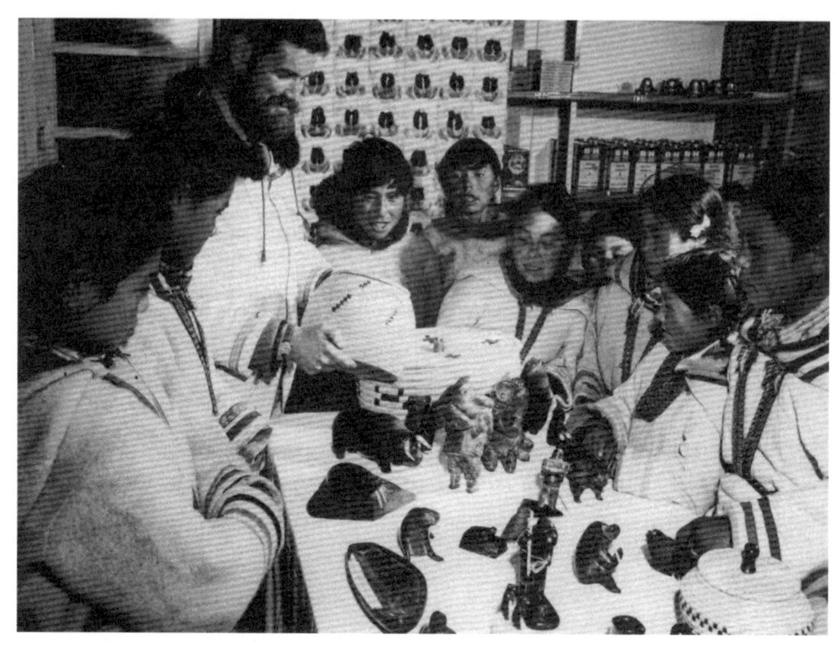

ESKIMOS AND HOUSTON EXAMINE CARVINGS
PANGNIRTUNG, BAFFIN ISLAND

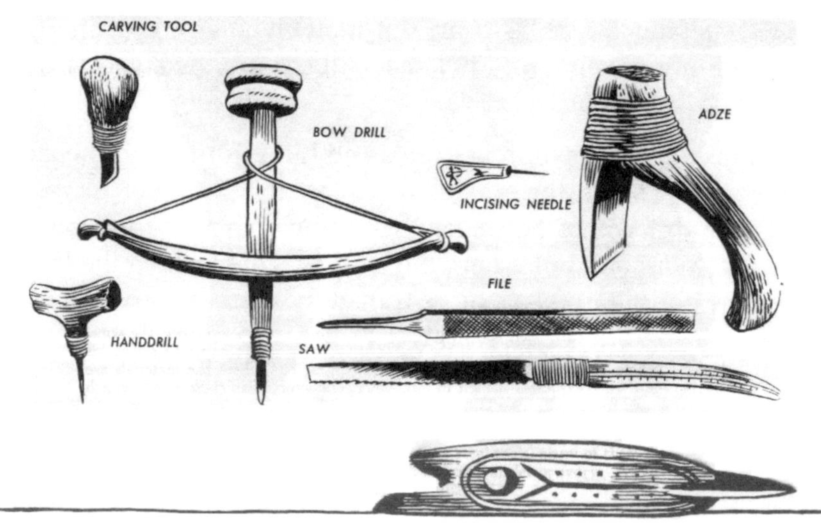

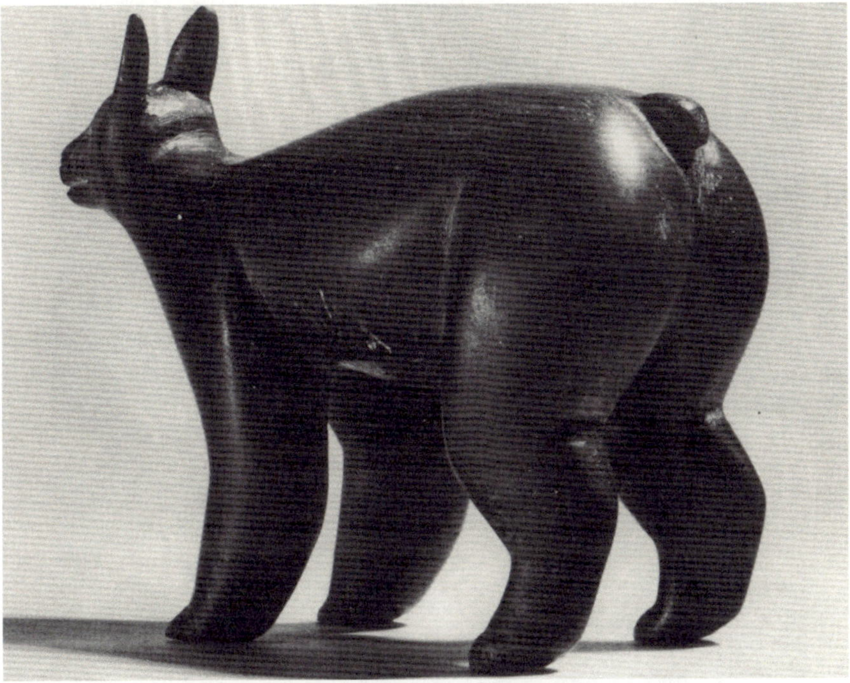

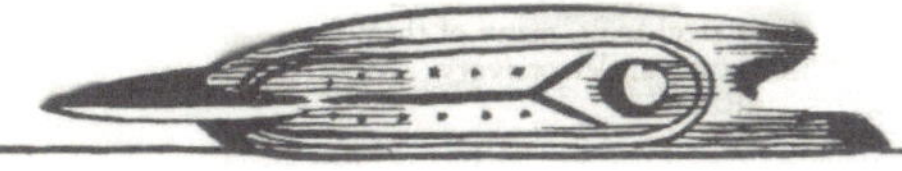

RABBIT BY KUMALIK, POVUNGNITUK
EAST COAST HUDSON BAY

THE MUSK-OX is an animal worthy of the Eskimo hunter. From earliest times it provided meat in lavish quantity, its horns made bows, its shaggy hair was warm. The musk-ox is honoured in Eskimo legend and song, and in carving. The carving is a tribute to its subject; and, the carver thinks, it may also be an encouragement to the musk-ox to present itself to the hunter.

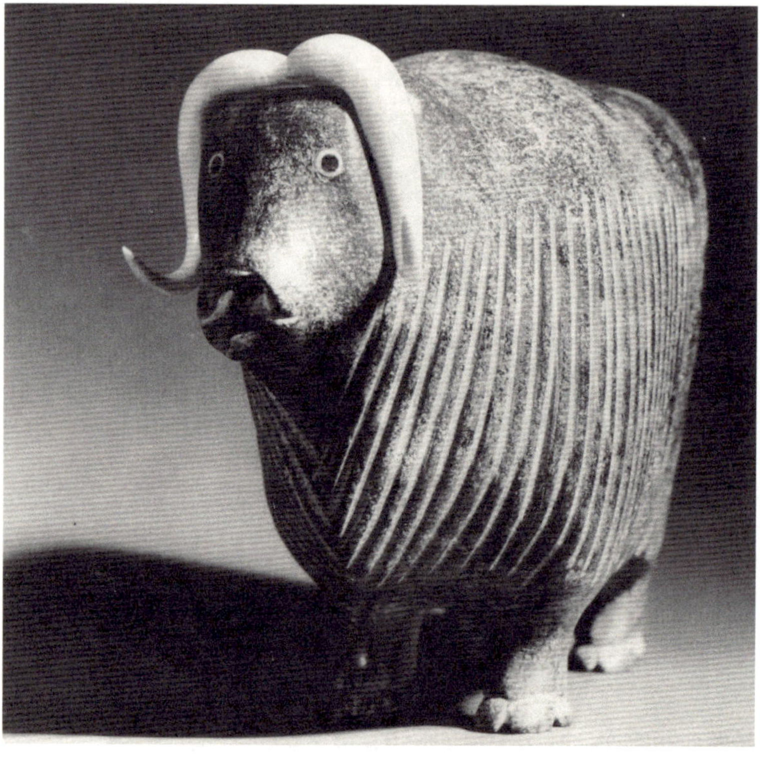

MUSK-OX BY AKEEATASHUK
CRAIG HARBOUR, ELLESMERE ISLAND

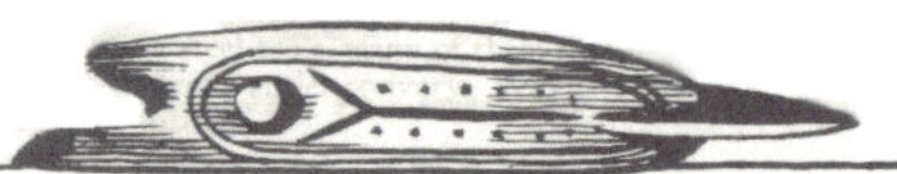

THE FISH, on other hand, is a lowly creature, fit to be caught only when other animals have disappeared. No Eskimo hunter wishes to be seen over a hole in the ice waiting for a rock cod to pass by when there should be bigger game worthy of his skill. With the same distaste does the artist regard all fish, and carvings of it are rare.

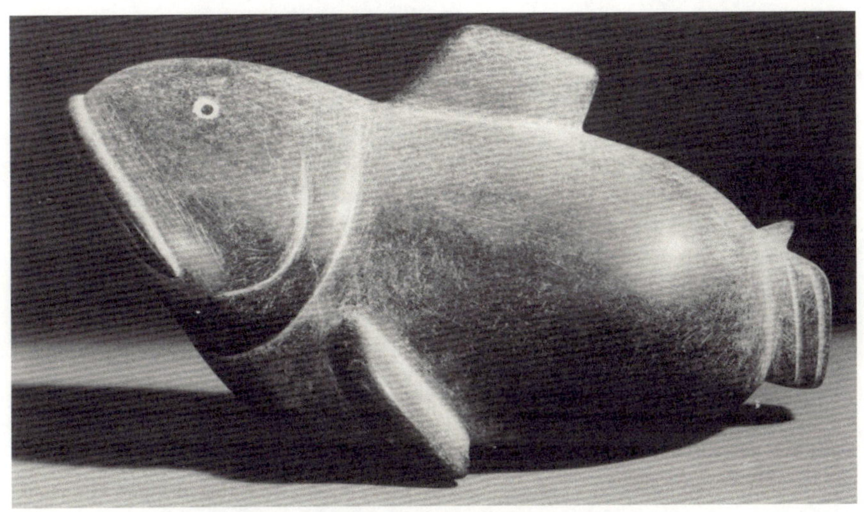

ROCK COD BY TUNU
CAPE DORSET, BAFFIN ISLAND

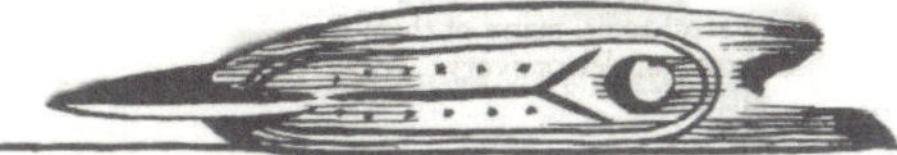

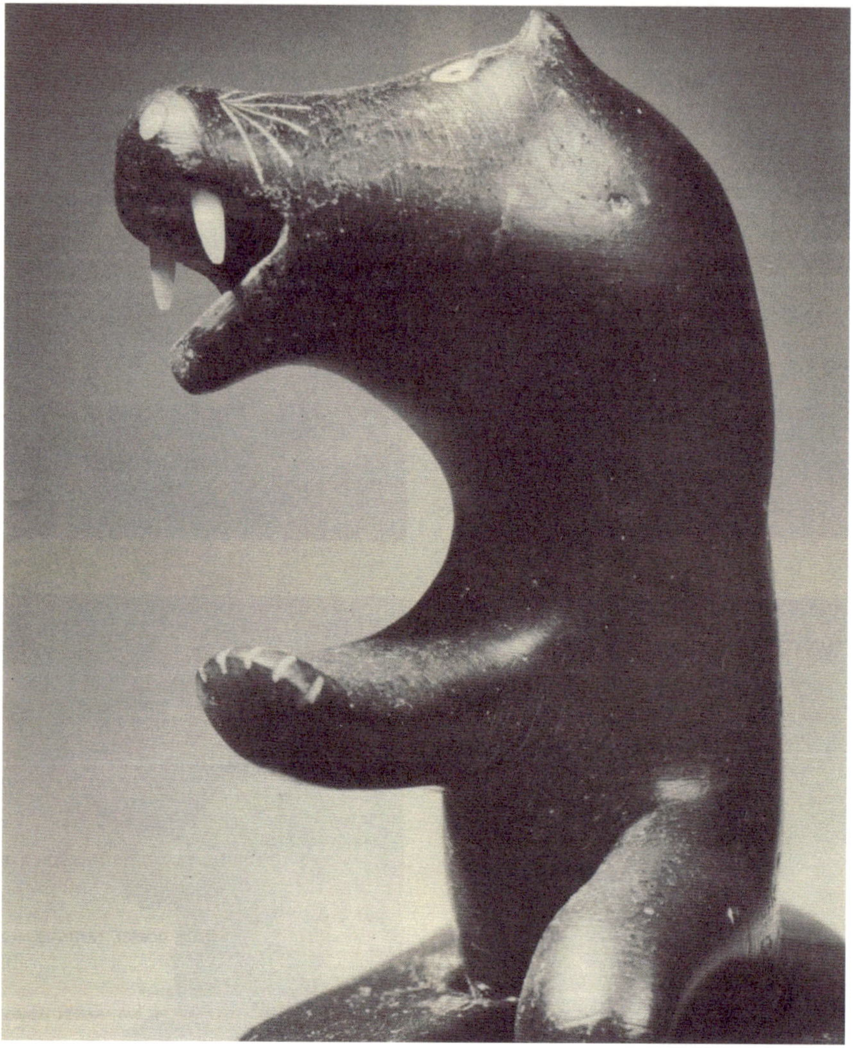

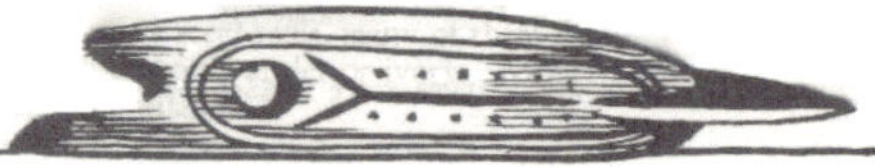

BADGER BY KALINGO
POVUNGNITUK, EAST COAST HUDSON BAY

EVEN THE BEST OF ESKIMO ARTISTS is a hunter first, a carver second. His very life depends on his keenness of observation, his consciousness of every feature, of every movement, of every habit of the animals which provide his food. He knows the subjects he carves with an intimacy which the sparseness of his life dictates.

Kalingo's rifleman depicts a basic concept – the hunter in action. Nothing of the scene is lost to him, but with his hard stone and his primitive tools he must choose conveyed with striking clarity and an economy of line. Sarkee's bear, rising from the water with a roar, has a force in action which could scarcely be surpassed in plastic form.

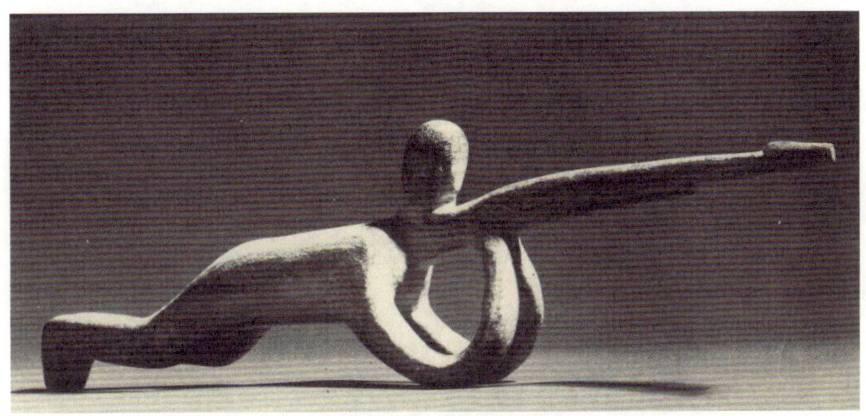

RIFLEMAN BY KALINGO
POVUNGNITUK, EAST COAST HUDSON BAY

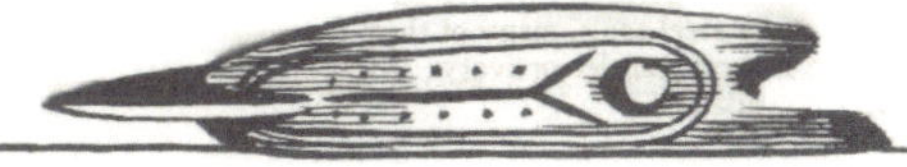

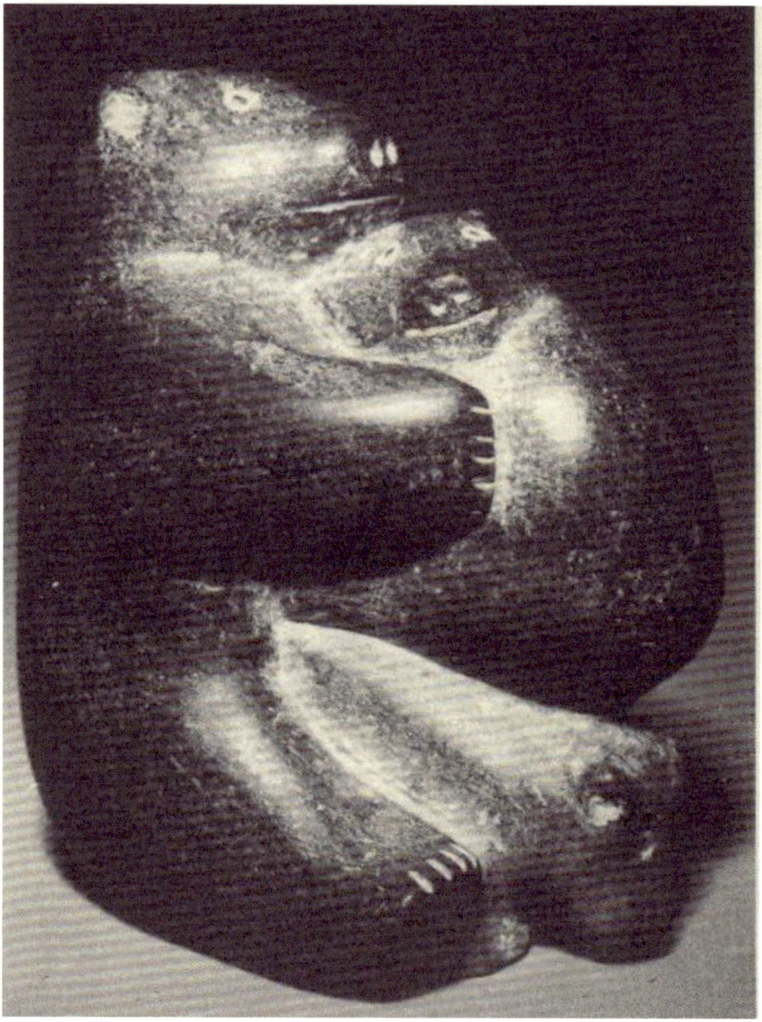

BEAR AND CUBS BY NAPACHEE
CAPE DORSET, BAFFIN ISLAND

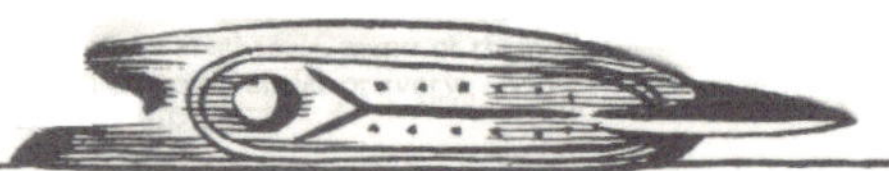

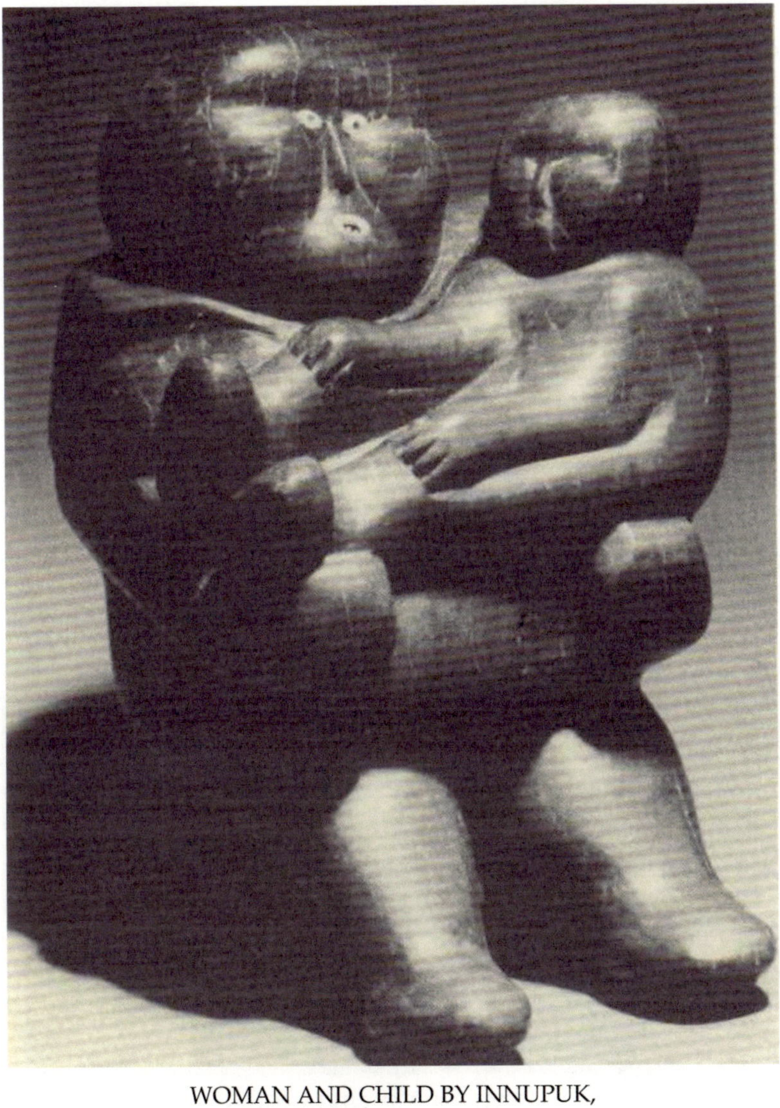

WOMAN AND CHILD BY INNUPUK,
PORT HARRISON, EAST COAST HUDSON BAY

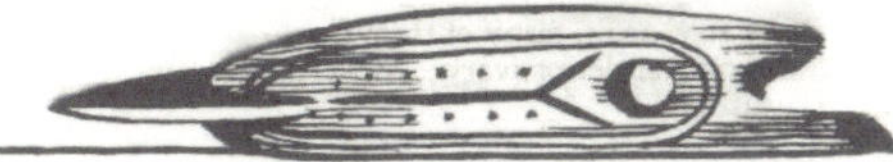

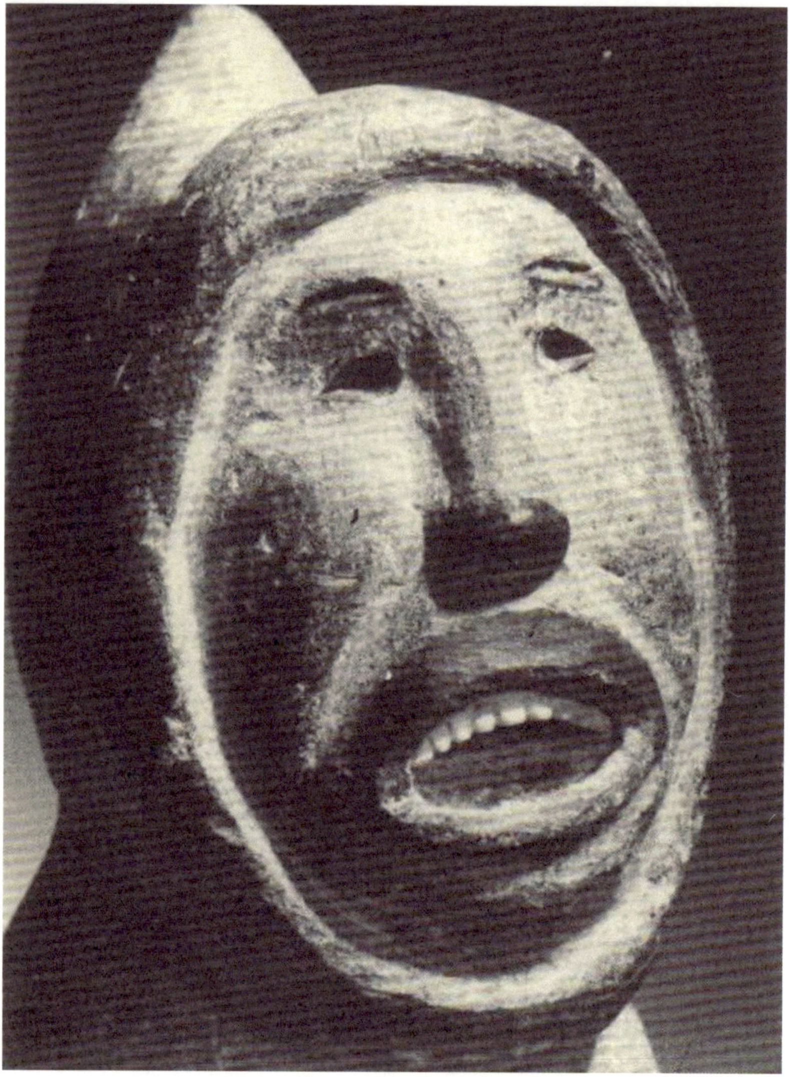

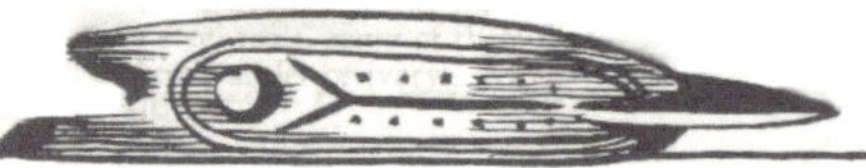

MAN'S HEAD BY NIVIAKCIAK
CAPE DORSET, BAFFIN ISLAND

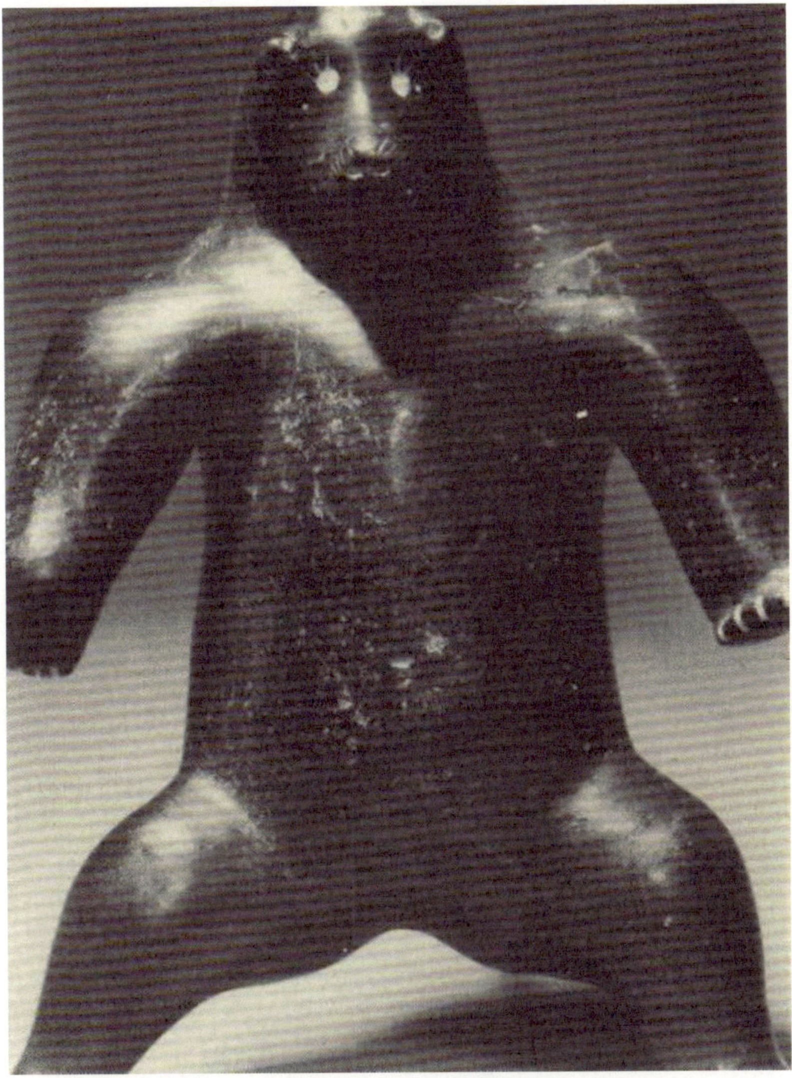

BEAR BY PILLIPUSSY
FORT HARRISON, EAST COAST HUDSON BAY

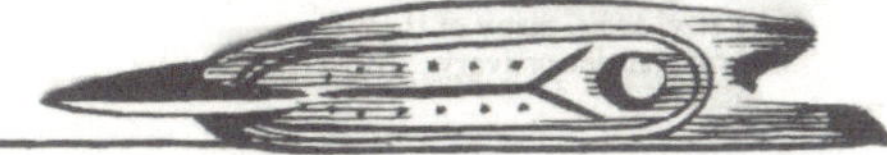

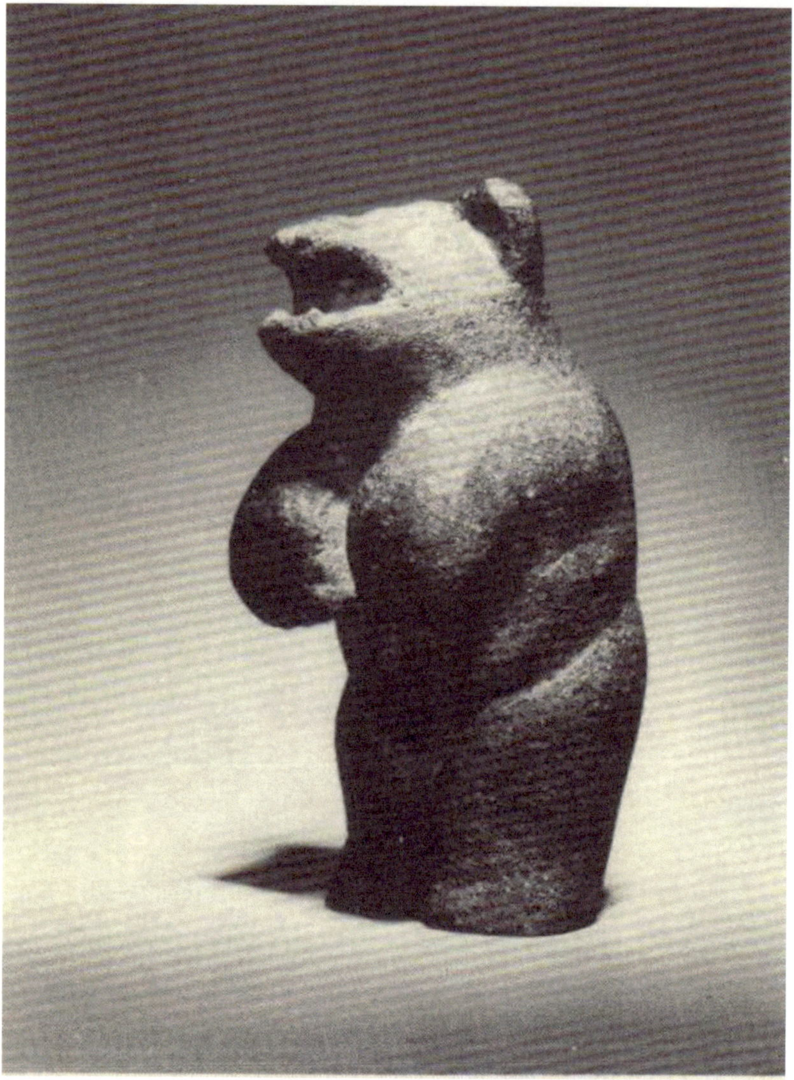

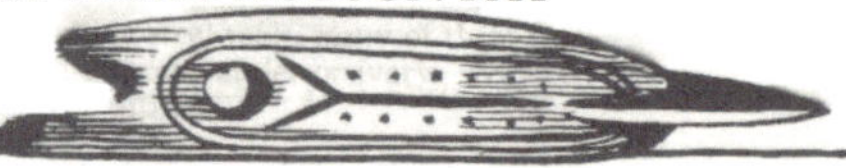

BEAR BY PILLIPUSSY
FORT HARRISON, EAST COAST HUDSON BAY

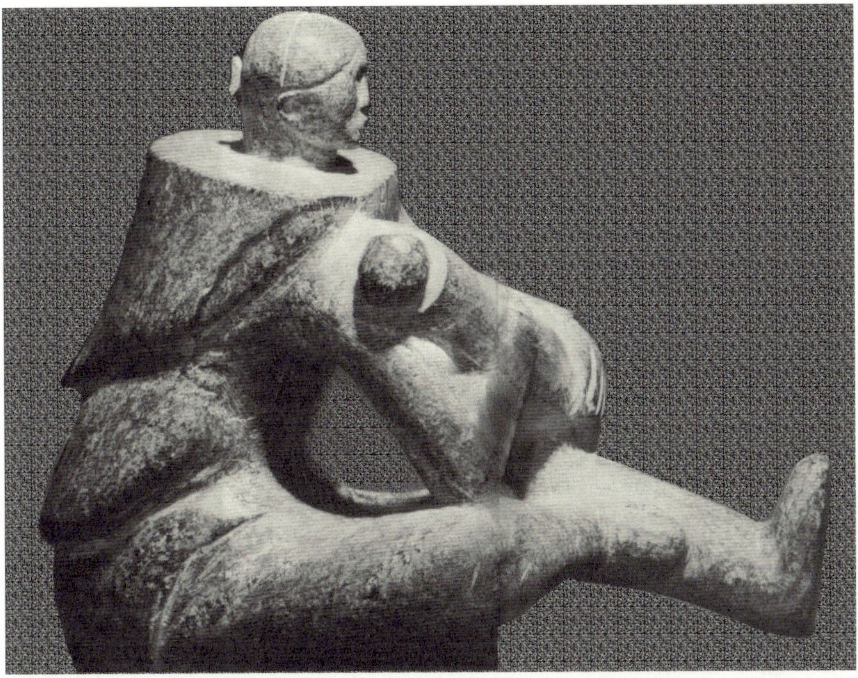

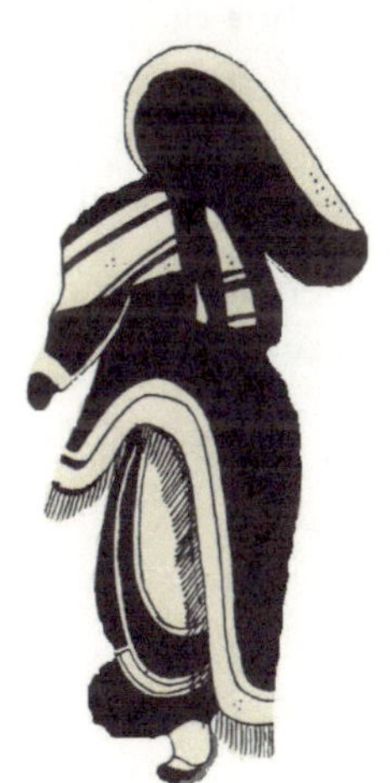

ESKIMO WOMAN, ARCTIC BAY, BAFFIN ISLAND

THE WOMEN'S ART

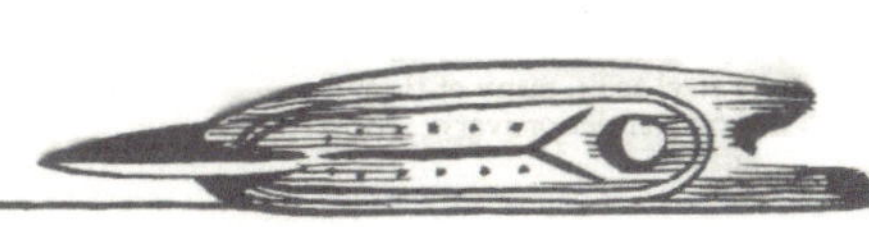

FEW WOMEN have inter-
ested themselves in carving.
Their artistic inclinations and
abilities find expression along
other lines. Beautiful clothing is
decorated with multitude of nar-
row inset strips of white or
brown fur; to make a single gar-

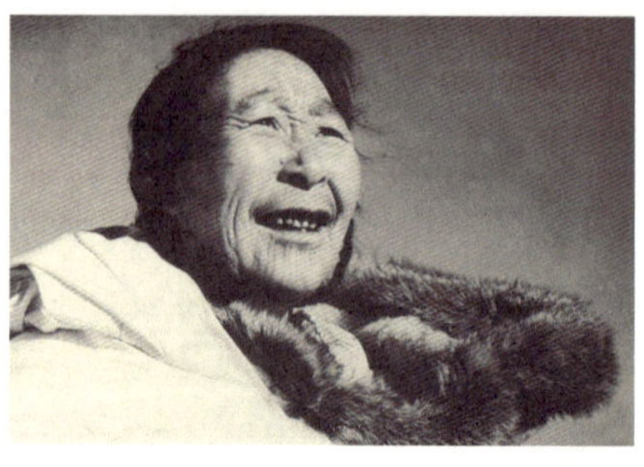

ment may require miles of careful stitching with an awl and sinew
in place of needle and thread. When beads became available, they
were used together with the fur insets, or sometimes instead of
them, but the basic designs were often followed.

But apart from all the decorative arts employed in their
clothing styles, there is another and more significant women's art,
one which seems to be created at times for magical reasons and at
other times simply as a mode of artistic expression – the skin
picture.

The background material of the picture is most often
bleached sealskin or caribou hide, usually an Eskimo woman
visualises her design in its entirety before she begins to sew, and
cuts out of objects without preliminary drawing or guide lines.
Like the men who carve, she relies completely upon memory of
form – an artistic feat in itself.

When the silhouettes are completed, they are superimposed
upon the white background following the preconceived pattern

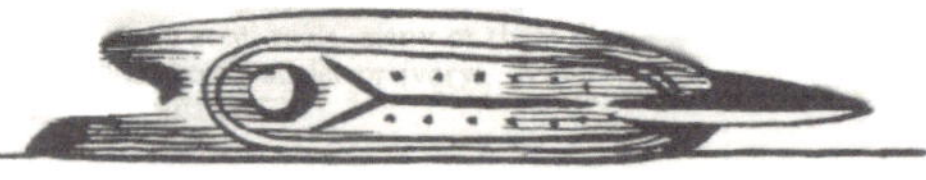

In the Eastern Arctic, cut-outs are made of thin, black sealskin and are stitched onto bags and other articles. Most of these cut-outs depict objects familiar to the woman who makes them – her ulu, the crescent shaped knife which is an almost universal tool in women's work, the adze her husband uses, the steel axe brought in by a trader, gloves, scissors, a comb, birds and beasts.

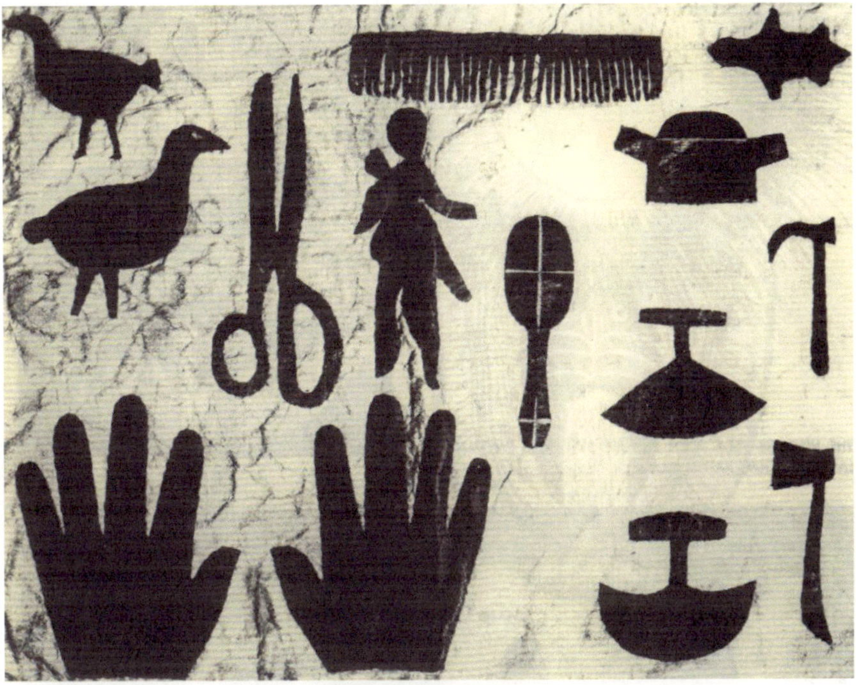

SEAL SKIN PICTURE BY KEAKJUK
CAPE DORSET, BAFFIN ISLAND

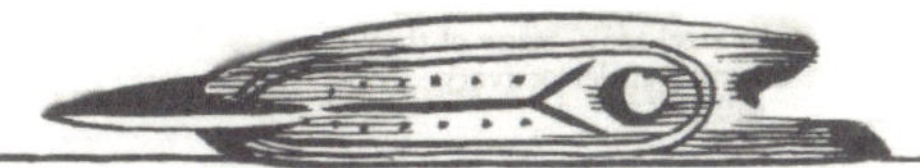

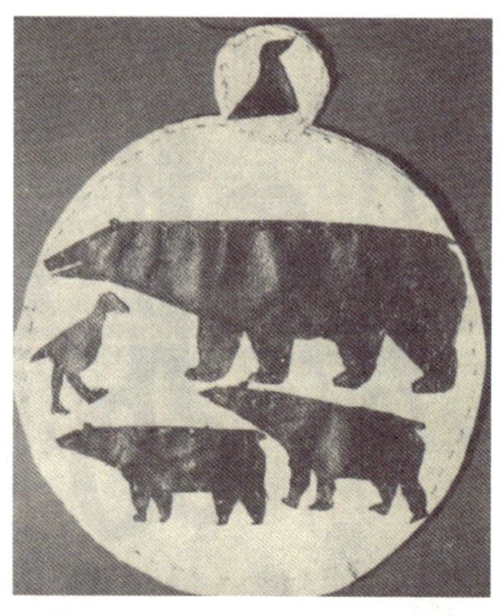

BEAR HUNT, SEAL SKIN PICTURE
BY PITSULAK (WOMAN)
TIKKEERAK, BAFFIN ISLAND

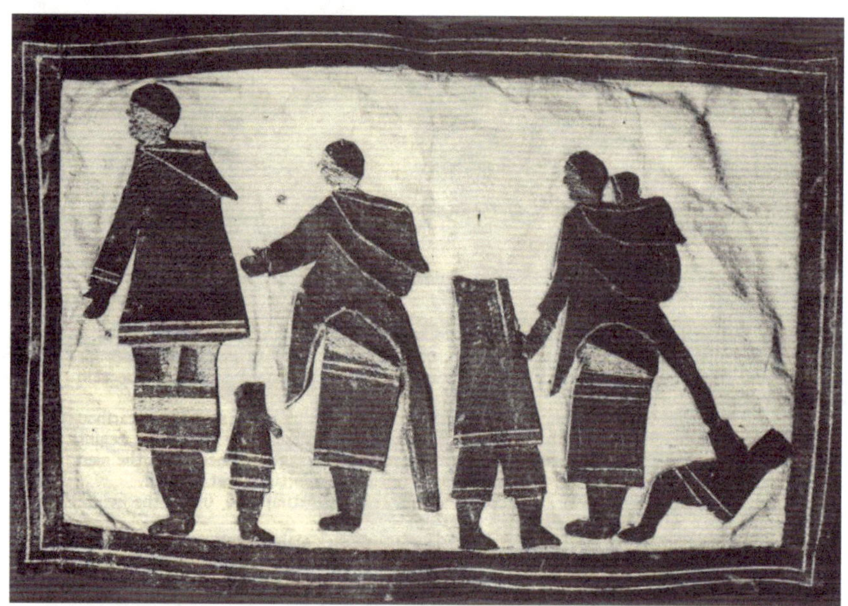

THE VISITORS – SEAL SKIN PICTURE BY JOSEE (WOMAN)
LAKE HARBOUR, BAFFIN ISLAND

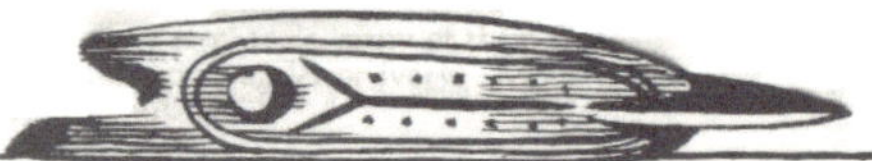

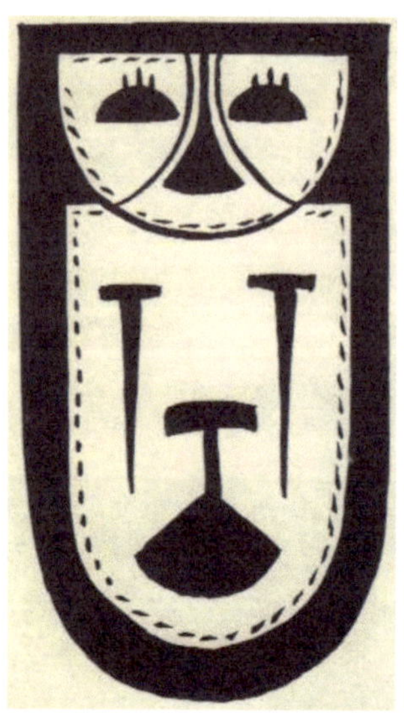

SLIPPER VAMP
REPULSE BAY, MELVILLE
PENINSULA

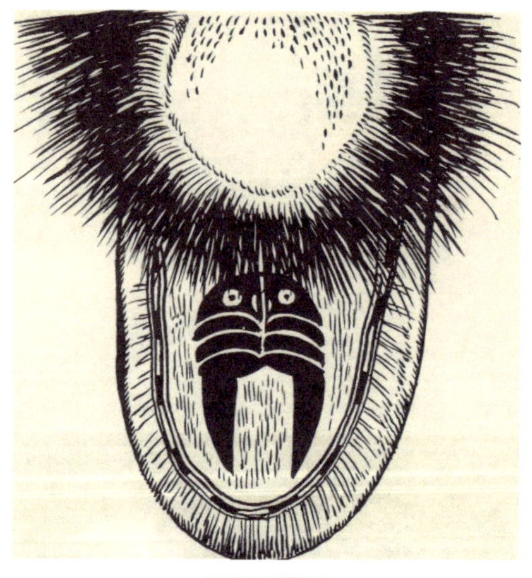

SLIPPER (SEALSKIN)
FROBISHER BAY, BAFFIN
ISLAND

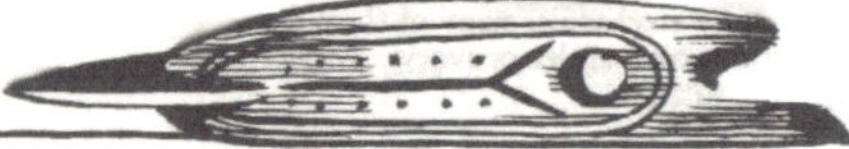

THOUGH FOR SUMMER wear woollen duffle from the trading post is becoming more widespread, the skin of the caribou or the seal remains the commonest material for clothing. It is tailored with imagination and superb craftsmanship, for an Eskimo woman earns respect for herself and her husband by the quality and design of her family's clothes. The skins, whose colours range from almost black to purest white, are carefully matched. Light horizontal strips are added for more than decoration: they give added strength to the garment. Skins of arctic animals and the head plumage of the eider duck are used for general decorations. Sealskin bags for carrying equipment may bear designs of cut-out skin. This general ornamentation is not functional; it is merely the Eskimo's love of colour and design in a country where the attractions of nature are simple and vast.

The grasses needed by the basket maker are not common throughout the Canadian Arctic; but particularly in the Eastern Arctic basket making is an old an established art. Here is the only part of Canada, excepting British Columbia, where the coil technique is used. Sealskin strips or the sinew of whale are woven into simple designs. The lid is often mounted with a small bone or ivory figure to serve as a handle.

The art of basketry is developed to its highest level among the Eskimos on the east coast of Hudson Bay. This is still the country of tundra, far north of the tree line, but lime grass grows in quantity along the river valleys.

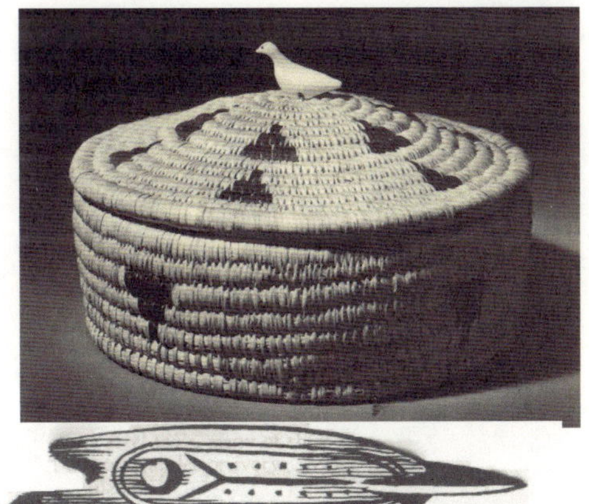

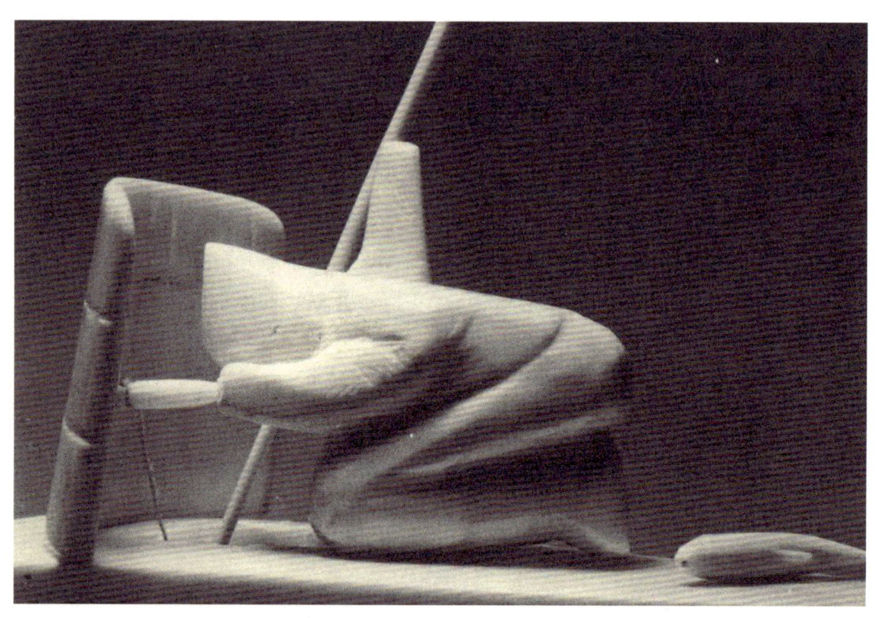

FISHING THROUGH THE ICE (IVORY) BY ANAWAK
REPULSE BAY, MELVILLE PENINSULA

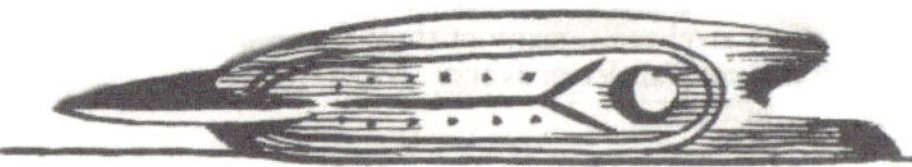

ESKIMO etiquette requires a display of modesty that the artist may not necessarily feel. The carver is likely to malign his own work, saying it is useless and worthless and that he should never try such a thing again. He is usually reluctant to copy or repeat a subject of his own, or indeed anybody else's work. This is fortunate, for I consequence he produces a wide variety of subject, no two pieces being alike in form, movement, or concept.

There is a curious convention in Eskimo art. When a swimming animal is depicted, only the part of its body visible above water is carved. A walrus emerging from the water, a bird rising to the surface with a fish in its beak, a polar bear plunging into the sea, all these carvings are cut off through a horizontal plane representing the surface of the water.

Why does the Eskimo carve? What induces people so hard pressed by their environment to expend energy in unessential occupation? It is impossible to know the objectives of the ancient Eskimo carvers since no written record accompanies their work. It is not easy either to analyse the motives of living Eskimo artists, because they seldom give utterance to abstract thought.

Quite naturally they enjoy the increased income that their art has provided in recent years. Fears have been expressed that is would lead to degeneration in the art form, but this has not been the case, nor is it likely to be. The Eskimo himself has already set standards for his art which he must maintain to command not only a market, but, more important, the respect of his fellow artists.

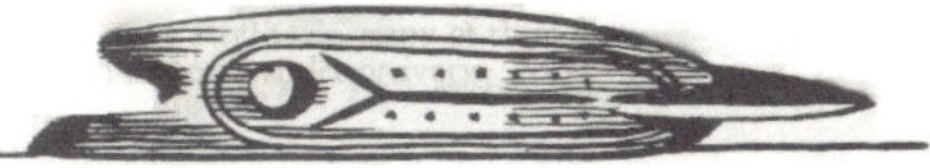

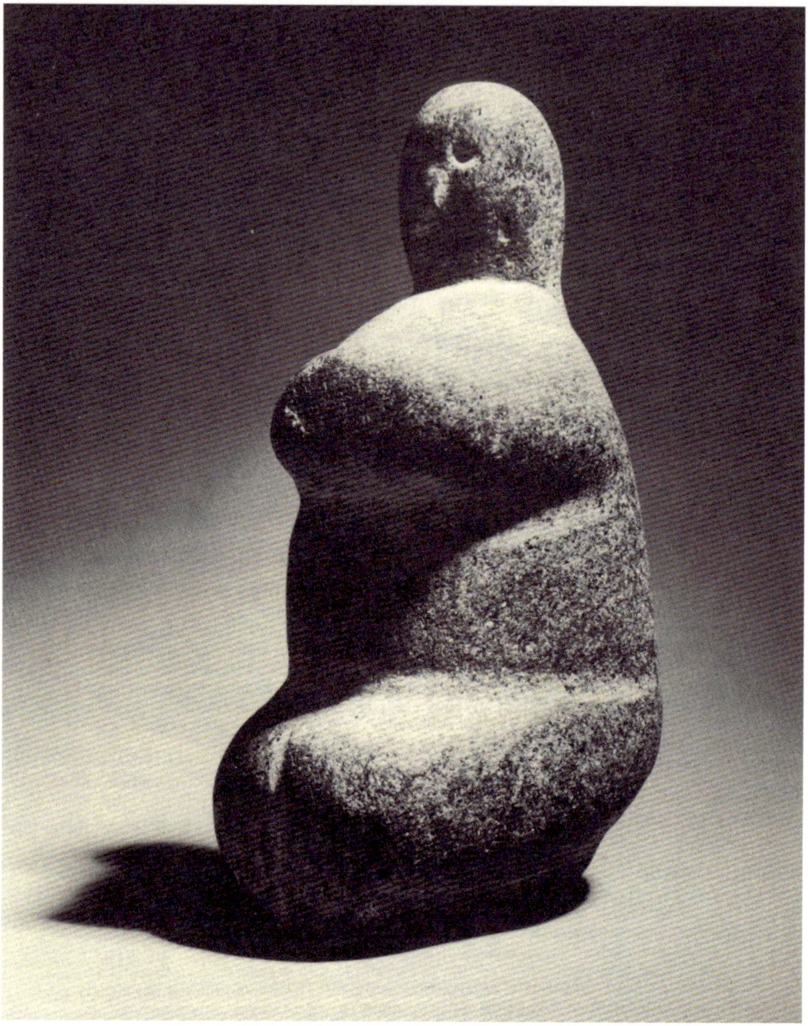

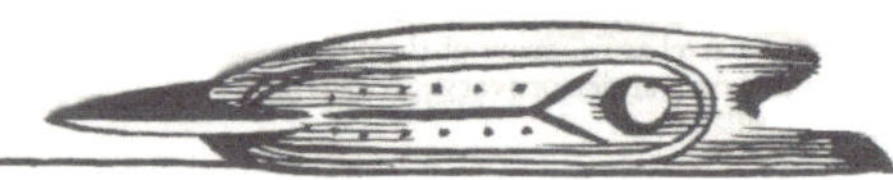

MAN KNEELING (GRANITE) BY TUDLIK
CAPE DORSET, BAFFIN ISLAND

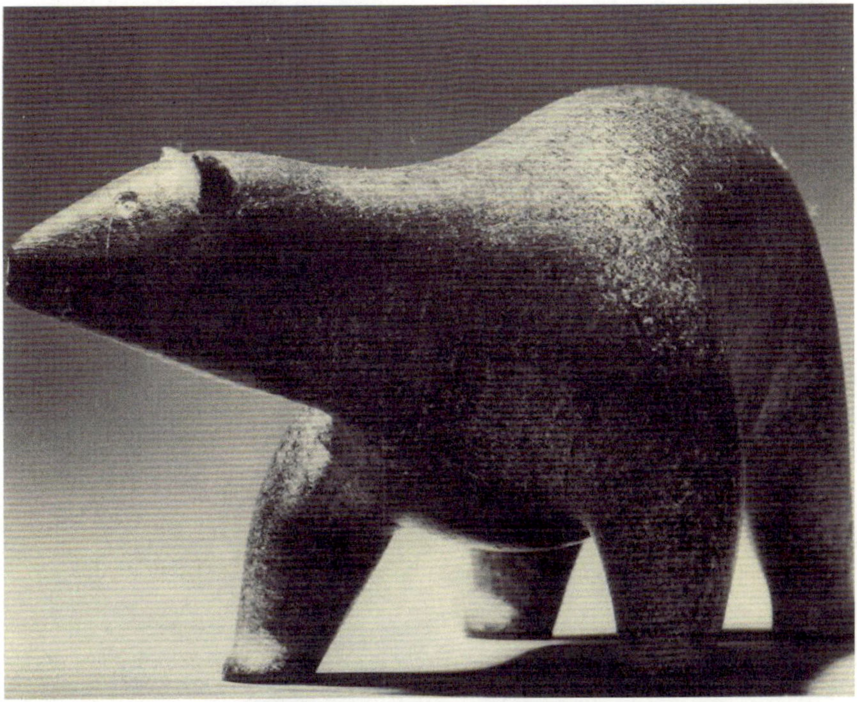

POLAR BEAR (STONE) BY TIKEETUK
KANDEAK, BAFFIN ISLAND

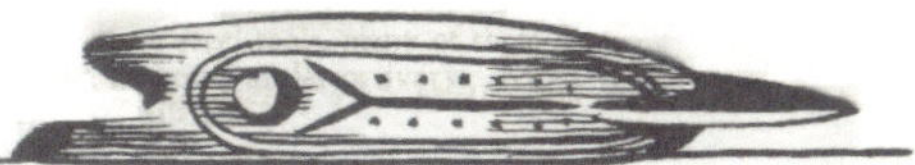

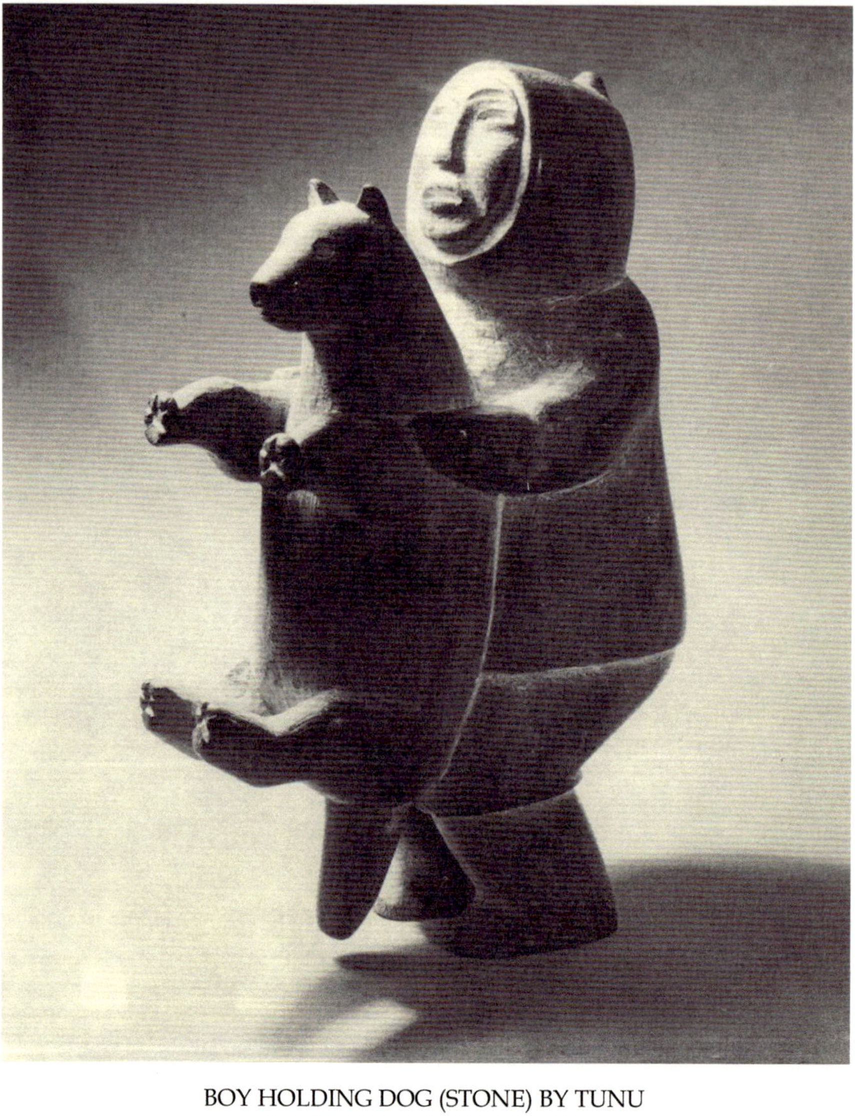

BOY HOLDING DOG (STONE) BY TUNU
KANDEAK, BAFFIN ISLAND

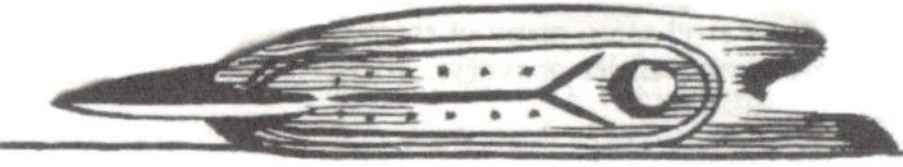

ONE Eskimo finds beauty in the light sleek lines of the weasel. Another sees the massive bulk of the walrus. Another tries to capture in stone the sullen treachery of a bear. They watch an infinity of detail, then, perhaps, discard all but the essence of the form. In quiet moments they remember, and carve what they see beyond the Arctic night. They carve without pretension and without self consciousness, for art has not yet become specialisation. It belongs to all.

What motivates this man in his art? Perhaps it is the clinging remnant of a forgotten civilisation, of the Asiatic continent where he almost certainly originated. Perhaps it is pure love of craftsmanship which he clearly holds in high esteem. The severe climate demands that the Eskimo spend much of his life in his home. He must provide his own amusement. His industrious habits leave him time to contemplate and perfect his art. And, of course, he has never wasted his energy on warfare.

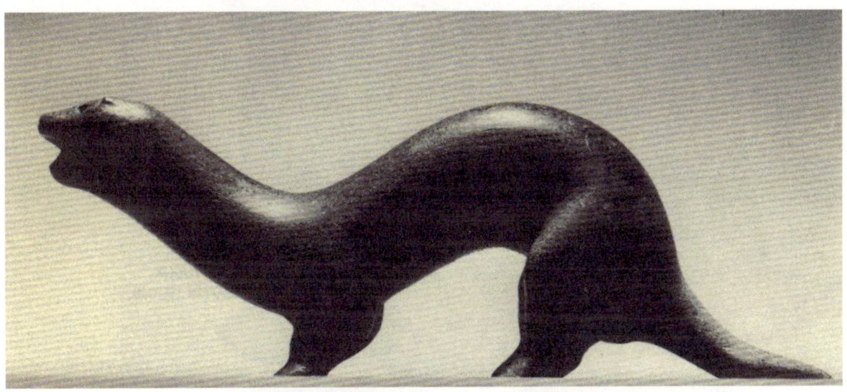

WEASEL (STEATITE) BY SHEROAPIK
POVUNGNITUK, EAST COAST HUDSON BAY

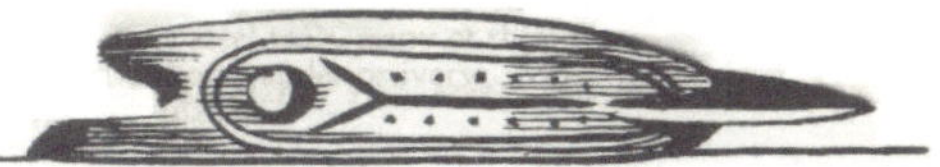

JUST before the hunt at Povungnituk, Kopeekolik carved a superb walrus in stone. It was tribute to the walrus, which might bring good fortune. He kept it hidden away, to be treasured quietly. He called himself a useless and clumsy carver, and only with reluctance would he produce his art. When he was asked to carve another, Kopeekolik was perplexed. After long silence he exclaimed, "You see that I can carve likeness of walrus! Why would you want another one?" He had proven himself a carver of walrus, and that was enough. But when the idea of carving a caribou was suggested to him, he immediately became excited. He had yet to prove himself a carver of caribou. And he went to find some stone.

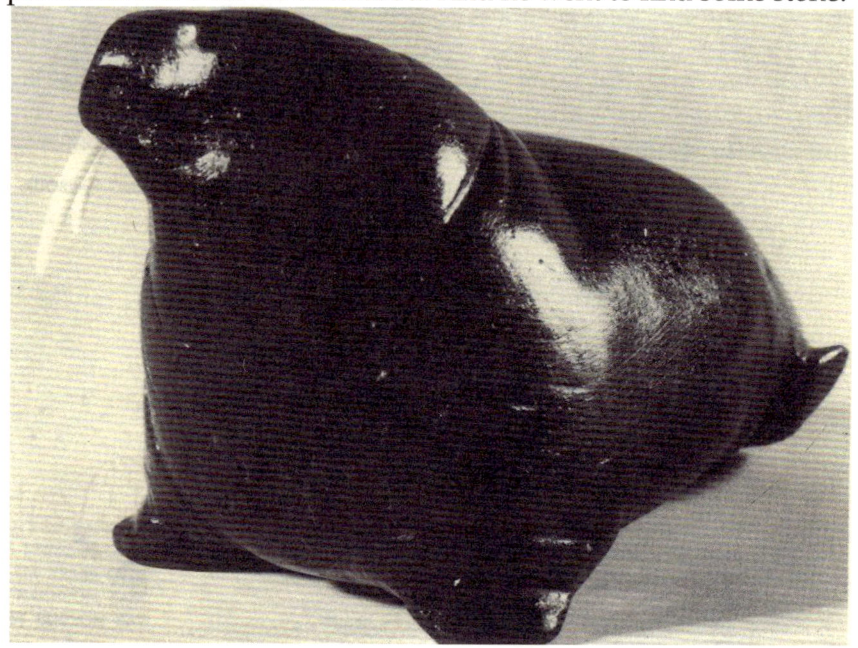

WALRUS (STEATITE) BY KOPEEKOLIK
POVUNGNITUK, EAST COAST HUDSON BAY

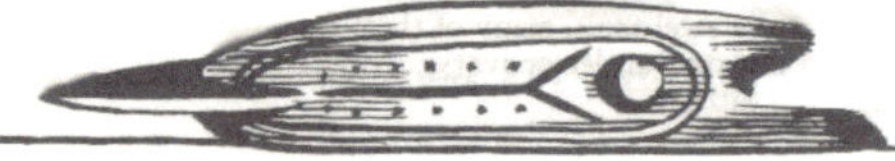

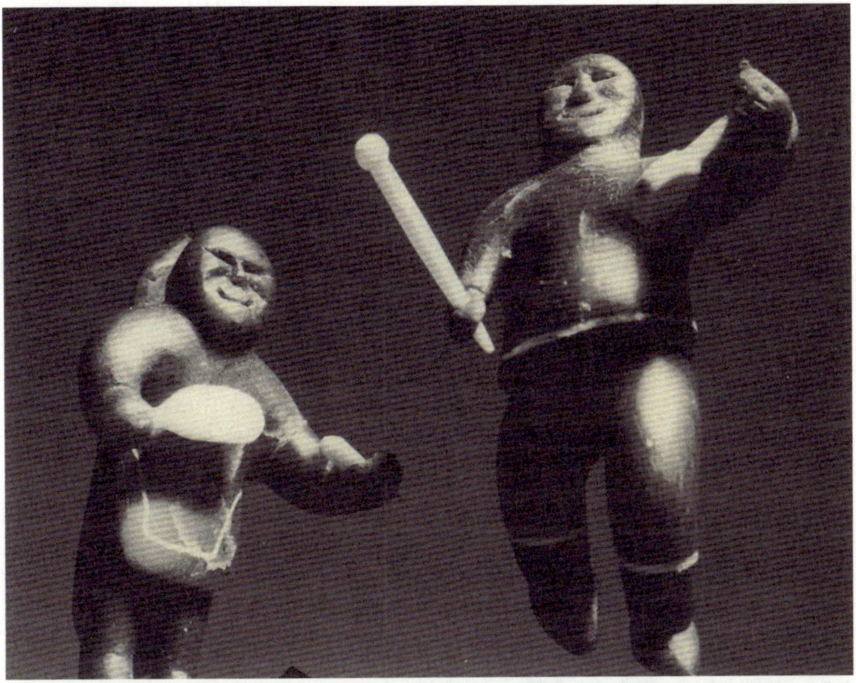

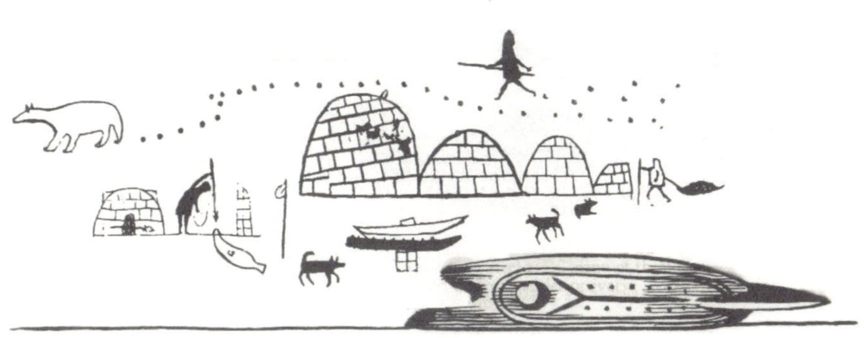

DRUM DANCERS (STONE) BY AKEEAKTASHUK
CRAIG HARBOUR, ELLESMERE ISLAND

CARVING, THE DECORATION OF SKINS, DRAW-
ING ON HORNS AND ANTLERS – these are the forms of
Canadian Eskimo Art which the outside world best knows. Sing-
ing, dancing and the poetry of the Eskimo legend or song are
equally a part of the culture, but they are lesser known for they
cannot be translated, or can be translated only with difficulty, to an
alien land and an alien tongue.

The carver, though, sometimes puts in stone the lively moments of the Eskimo dance. His sculpture suggests the mechanics
of a music which is solemn, even mournful to unfamiliar ears, but
as subtly expressive of the Eskimo's reaction to his world as the
most vivid carving.

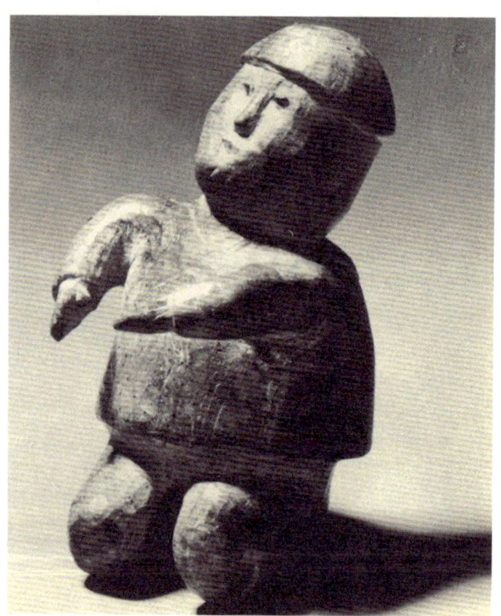

SMALL BOY DANCING ON
HIS KNEES (STONE), BY
KUNI (14 YEARS OLD)
PORT HARRISON, EAST
COAST HUDSON BAY

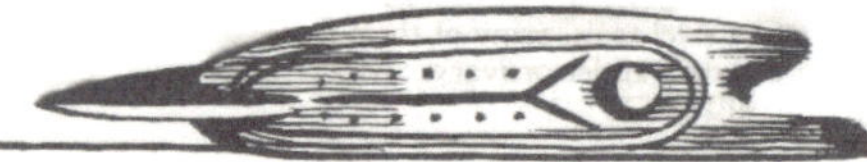

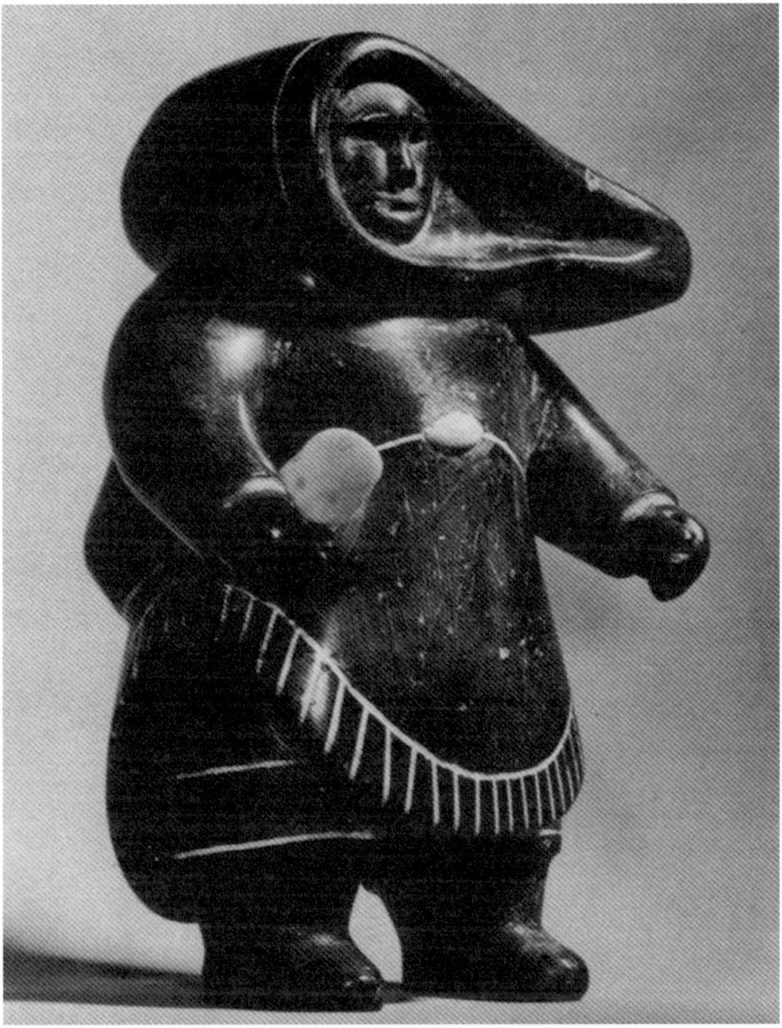

WOMAN IN THE WIND BY AKEEAKTASHUK
CRAIG HARBOUR, ELLESMERE ISLAND

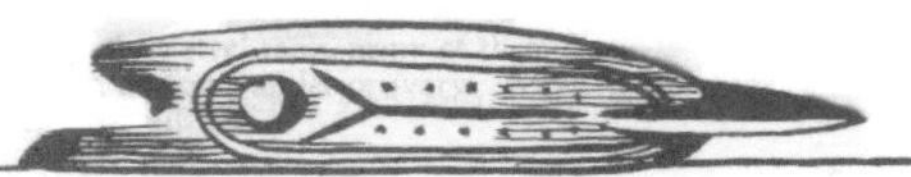

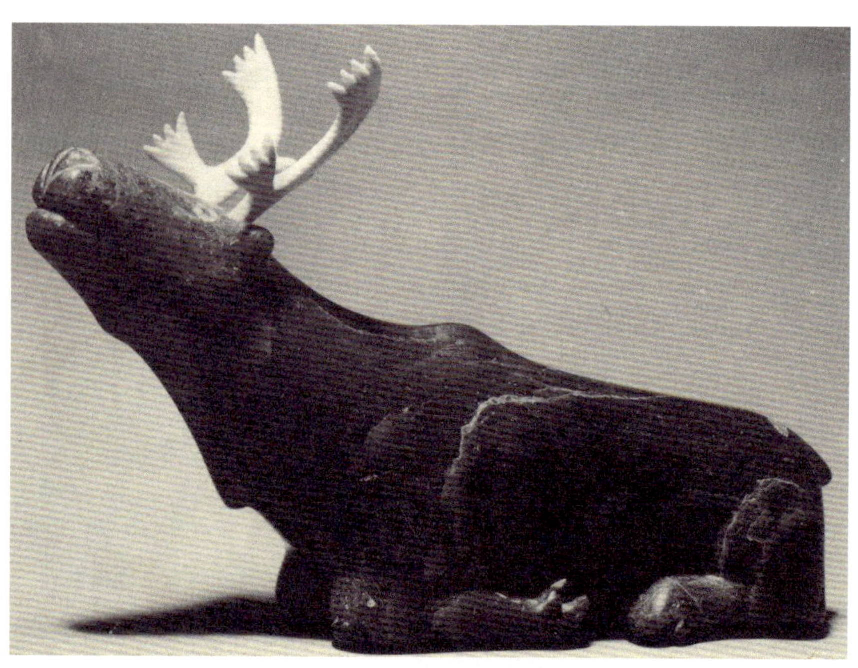

CARIBOU BY AMIDILAK
KOGALUK RIVER, EAST COAST HUDSON BAY

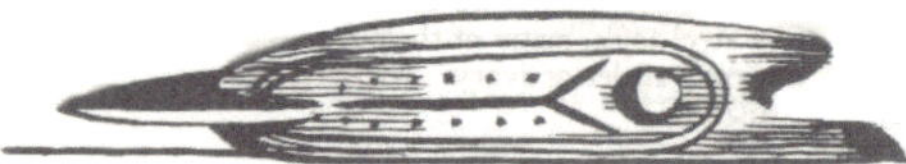

IT IS DIFFICULT TO DISCOVER what precise aesthetic satisfaction their art has for the Eskimos themselves. It is known, however,
that some of the small carvings found in the ancient villages had
magical significance. This, of course, is a familiar concept in early
art forms. In primitive minds throughout the world the idea has
persisted that to make likeness of anything helps to materialise it.
The primitive magician has, since early
times, painted, drawn, or modelled images of the animals on which
he and his tribesmen depend for food. Perhaps the
Eskimo hunter still attaches magical significance to the
little models of the game he hopes to kill.

Other carvings, many of them representing
inanimate objects, were made to be put on the graves of
the dead. A model sled, kayak, or harpoon on a man's
grave; miniature cooking pots, lamps and sewing kits
on a woman's grave, would serve the deceased just as
well in the land of spirits as would their
originals, which were usually
too valuable to the living to
be lavished on the dead.

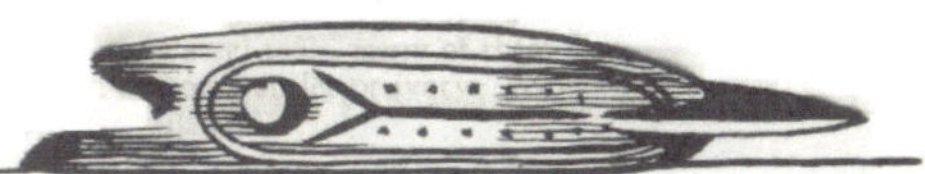

AN ESKIMO CARVING is made to be examined at close quarters, to be touched and fondled. It is not intended to be put on a pedestal and examined from a respectful distance. Since it is small, it can be passed from hand to hand while friends and visitor exclaim and comment, admire and praise the artist. For this reason every aspect of the object such as the paws of a bear, the underparts of a caribou are carefully carved and polished. When it is finished, it is wrapped and put away in a piece of soft skin. It will be produced again only when a visitor arrives.

The art of the Eskimo is personal, created for the artist's satisfaction, not just for commercial ends. So it must remain. The Canadian Government and the Canadian Handicrafts Guild wish above all that this art should continue to flourish as a strong, fresh,

unspoiled impression of these vigorous people of the Canadian north. They hope, however, to provide the means for the Eskimo to share his artistry with the world he never sees.

But to the Eskimo carving will remain a simple thing, an accomplishment to be belittled before friends, a possession to be treasured only privately, an object to be shown when a visitor inquires: "Has one made any new carvings lately?"

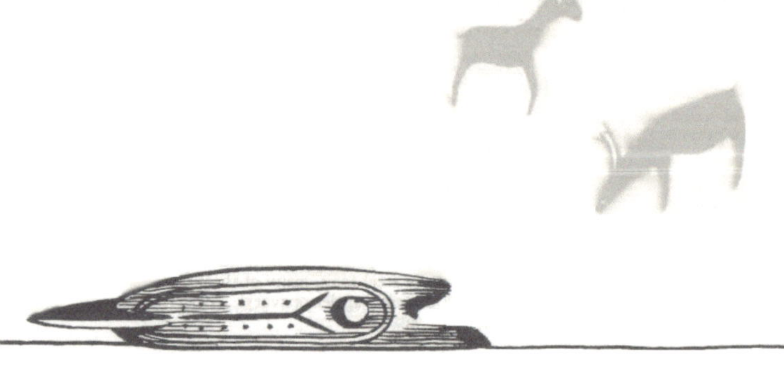

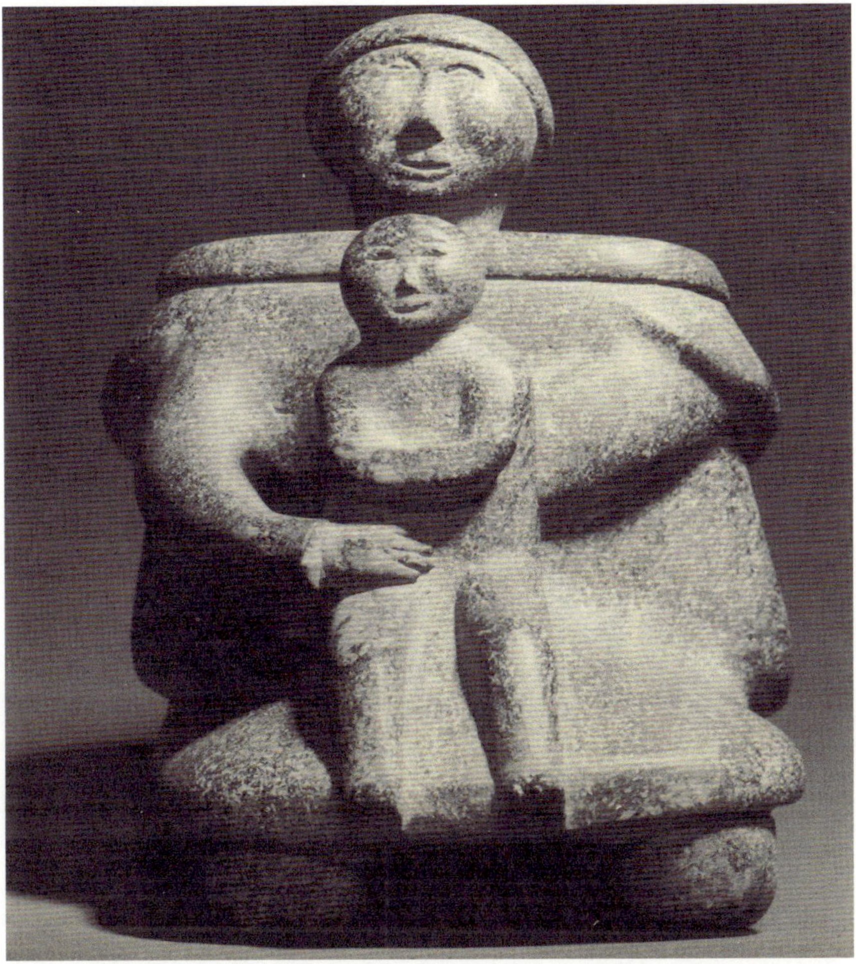

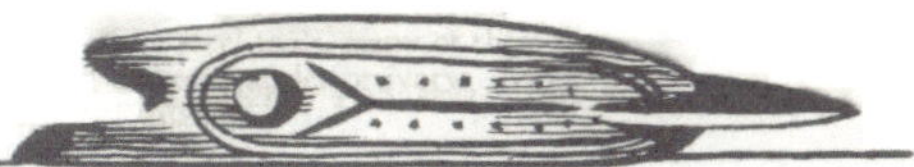

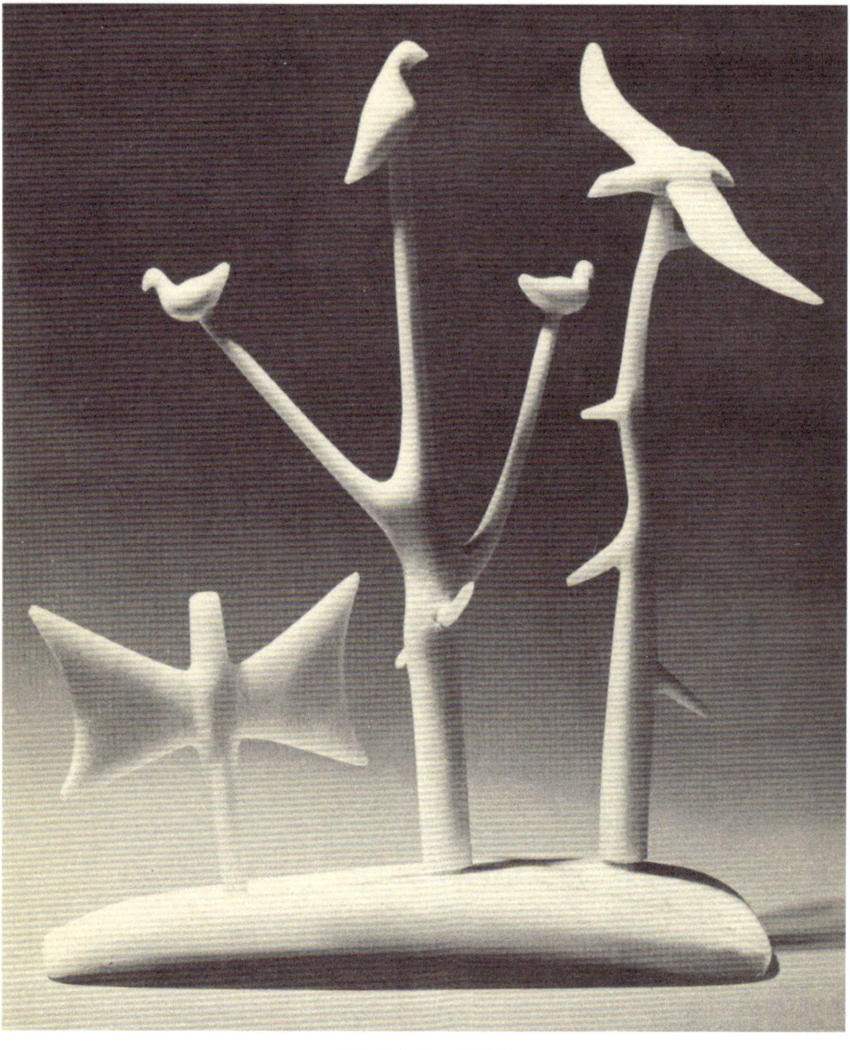

BIRDS IN A TREE
ITTORCHIAK, FROBISHER BAY, BAFFIN ISLAND

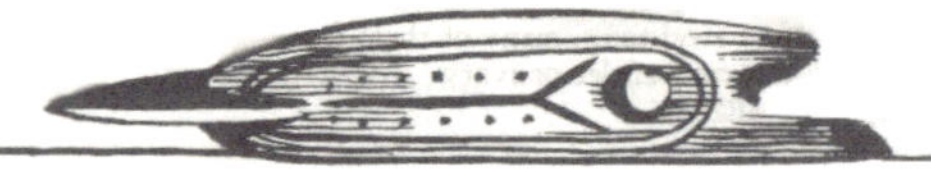

ESKIMO SONGS

As Translated by Tegoodligak, South Baffin Island

Aii

I think over again my adventures

When with the wind I drifted in my kayak

And thought I was in danger

My fears

Those small ones that seemed so big

For all the vital things

I had to get and to reach

And yet there is only one great thing

The only thing

To live to see the great day that dawns

And the light that fills the world.

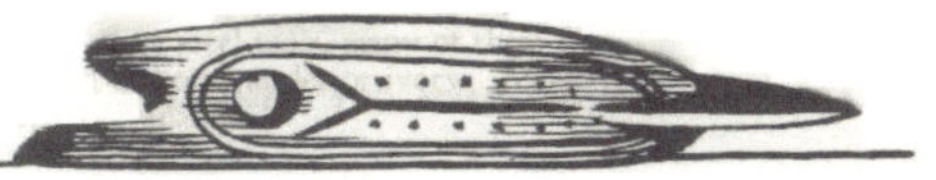

Aii

The Great sea has set me in motion

Set me adrift

And I move as a weed in the river

The Arch of sky

And mightiness of storms

Encompasses me

And I am left

Trembling with joy.

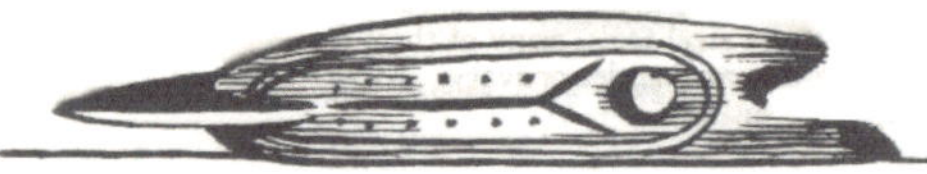

Aii

I walked on the ice of the sea

Wondering I heard

The song of the sea

And the great sighing

Of the new formed ice

Go then go

Strength of soul

Brings health

To the place of feasting.

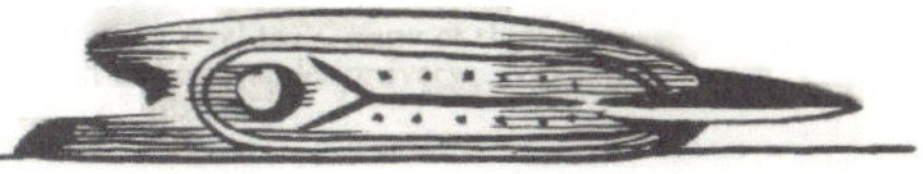

Aii

I return to my little song

And patiently I sing

Above fishing holes in the ice

Else I too quickly tire

When fishing upstream

When the wind blows cold

Where I stand shivering

Not giving myself time to wait for them

I go home saying

It was the fish that failed – upstream.

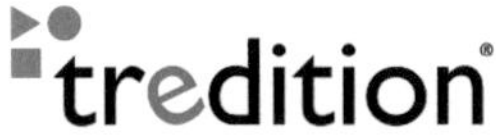

www.tredition.de

Über tredition

Der tredition Verlag wurde 2007 in Hamburg gegründet und ermöglicht Autoren das Publizieren von e-Books, audio-Books und print-Books. Autoren veröffentlichen ihre Bücher selbständig oder auf Wunsch mit der Unterstützung von tredition. print-Books sind in allen Buchhandlungen sowie bei Online-Händlern gedruckter Bücher erhältlich. e-Books und audio-Books können auf Wunsch der Autoren neben dem tredition Web-Shop auch bei weiteren führenden Online-Portalen zum Verkauf angeboten werden.

Auf www.tredition.de veröffentlichen Autoren in wenigen leichten Schritten ihr Buch. Zusätzlich bieten zahlreiche Literatur-Partner (das sind Lektoren, Übersetzer, Hörbuchsprecher und Illustratoren) ihre Dienstleistung an, um Manuskripte zu verbessern oder die Vielfalt zu erhöhen. Autoren können dieses Angebot nutzen und vereinbaren unabhängig von tredition mit Literatur-Partnern ihre Zusammenarbeit und partizipieren gemeinsam am Erfolg des Buches.